The Will to Power

Estrelda Y. Alexander

Seymour Press
Capitol Heights, MD

Image: Greg Rakozy

Printed in the United States of America

ISBN-13: 978-1938373398

Library of Congress Control Number: 2020934643

Seymour Press
Capitol Heights, MD

DEDICATION

To the brave young men of color, women of every age and culture, and all persons in every context who have been marginalized by the plethora of isms that challenge full human flourishing. And to those who are looking for the courage to speak when the burdensome weight of silence seems no longer an appropriate answer.

Table of Contents

ACKNOWLEDGMENTS

To all of those who have patiently listened while I wrestled through the issues in this volume. And to my good friend and colleague, Dr. Rosa Sailes for encouraging me to embrace the radical passion for justice within me that has been like "fire shut up in my bones." Had it not been for her, I do not know if I would have been brave enough to complete this project. To Dr. Lewis Brogdon, my student who is always pushing me to be the best teacher I could be and to openly share my voice with the world. And to Dr. Douglas Strong, my mentor and friend who first acknowledged that had something worthwhile to say and challenged me to say it with excellence in every instance.

FOREWORD

For decades–perhaps even centuries, some Christian preachers have overstressed the unworthiness of individuals to the point where people feel deeply ashamed or despicable. Citing certain biblical verses out of context and without any qualification (for example, Job 25:4, 6: "How can a mortal be righteous before God… a human being, who is a worm?"), such preachers have repeatedly emphasized our inadequacies and the multiple ways in which we don't deserve grace. While most of these preachers note that there is a remedy for spiritual inadequacy, found in Christ, they also make it clear to their hearers that this remedy only comes at the tremendous cost of Jesus' unfathomable suffering and death–due to our wickedness as human beings. Particular views of atonement (Christ's work on the cross) accentuate this emphasis on our failings and shortcomings.

Making matters worse, people who exercise power over others have often used such reasoning to keep marginalized folks in their place. In the nineteenth century U.S., for instance, white slave owners and their apologists explicitly employed religious arguments to justify the ongoing oppression of African Americans. Later, similar arguments were used to justify Jim Crow segregation. Blacks who heard such messages often internalized these false claims, resulting in self-loathing. Some churches in the U.S. have continued this type of theologizing up to the present, causing people–and especially people of color–to feel inferior.

One of the worst examples of this tendency occurred in Germany during the 19th and early 20th centuries. The German state church–called in Prussia (northern Germany) "The Evangelical Union Church" demanded total submission from its citizen-parishioners. Lower class people, in particular, were obliged to accept their fate and their demeaned status in society. Theological arguments reinforced these claims. The Prussian government, under a succession of kings and emperors (Kaisers), became ruthless rulers who controlled both state and church.

A number of university scholars drew attention to the religious complicity with state control in Germany. The philosopher Ludwig Feuerbach stated that religion was being used by powers-that-be to keep common people down. Dominant authorities remade God (who—according to Feuerbach–did not actually exist) into their own image, a kind of super-human who must be obeyed. Building on Feuerbach's ideas, Friedrich Nietzsche wrote about the way in which religious elements in society conspired with political leaders to create a master-slave mentality that deliberately sought to weaken people's ability to speak out against their own oppression. Nietzsche described how authorities used their power over and against exploited people, who were made weak by their religious sensibilities. The dominant class's will to power could be overcome only when those who were previously oppressed arose and asserted their own.

Nietzsche died in 1900. During the century following his death, many scholars—including numerous theologians—built on his argument that abused people could forcibly resist their exploitation by their will to power. While disavowing Nietzsche's atheism, these theologians agreed with his critique of Christianity, especially in those instances when religious leaders have affirmed and buttressed the dominant culture. Consequently, diverse types of theological liberalism (not to be confused with political liberalism) and, later, some of the contextual theologies, sought to minimize any theological claim that spoke about personal sin. Theological liberals and their heirs were convinced that preaching about human depravity—an emphasis that prevailed among theologically conservative Christians—kept the masses in a state of self-deprecation. Instead of human sinfulness, liberal theologians stressed the potential for human benevolence, through education and consciousness raising. In the U.S., a social gospel (closely connected to theological liberalism) developed to counter the hyper-individualism perceived in the personalized gospel (closely connected to fundamentalism) and lift up the voices of the marginalized.

Thirty-three years after Nietzsche's death, Nazism took hold in Germany, and Hitler pursued an even more aggressive posture than the earlier nineteenth century German despots regarding the role of governmental power over the rights of the individual. Hitler arrogantly asserted his struggle ("Mein Kampf") for domination, based on nationalism and racial pride. Ethnic diversity represented weakness, and that could be overcome only by asserting the supremacy of one race over another. Part of Nazi domination required the church's obeisance to the Reich, insisting that church leaders affirm a version of Nietzsche's master-slave mentality, which took the form of a state-sanctioned "German Christianity." A few bold Christians stood against this ethical compromise, especially a group of pastors and professors known as the "Confessing Church." The Confessing Church included people such as Dietrich Bonhoeffer, Martin Niemoeller, and Karl Barth. These Confessing pastors continued to preach and write from the standpoint of traditional theology, though with some new emphases, referred to as "neo-orthodoxy." Basing their theologizing on this neo-orthodox perspective, they spoke out forcefully about the idolatry of racial superiority and the need to sustain and support all people who find themselves on the edge.

Barth's articulation of "eccentricity" was perhaps the best example of lifting up the marginalized while still affirming an orthodox understanding of the faith. He wrote that "the human person, experiencing the power of the divine… cannot exist for [self alone]… but awakened to genuine humanity… also exists eccentrically"[1] Christians can welcome those who are different from us because our spiritual union with Christ impels us to move beyond ourselves toward others. Just as Christ does not exist for himself but extends himself for the sake of human beings, so Christian believers are truly human when we move outside of our own self-centeredness.[2] To be fully human, we step outside of the circle of ourselves to bring others into the larger circle of human flourishing. Eccentricity is the very nature of Christ, and thus should be for us.

Other twentieth century liberal and contextual theologians, however, were less careful to affirm orthodoxy, and in fact, openly rejected the evangelical call to personal confession and repentance—falsely blaming it for all the excesses of domineering political powers. In the Nietzschian sense, they became convinced that any stress on individual sin perpetuates oppression. Twentieth century liberal theology thus demonstrated a classic case of throwing the baby out with the bath water: they repudiated personal views of sin and salvation while accentuating social and systemic understandings—rather than seeing that both personal and social redemption are necessary.

Estrelda Alexander's compelling book forthrightly moves into this space. She names the will to power that affects all Christians. She exposes the pervasiveness of sin—both social and personal. People who exercise dominance over others express the will to power most obviously, and their entrenched biases must be confronted and denounced. But the will to power is also found among those who have been out of power and then begin to assert it. Alexander asks all Christians to recognize the degree to which we are prone to be duped by the subtle creep of power. Everyone views him or herself as better than some other person. Due to common human frailty, she states, all

---

1 Barth, Karl. *Church Dogmatics,* IV, 2, 547-48.

2 Phil 2. 3-8

of us are implicated, all of us are idolatrous, all of us seek to raise our own identity to a status above others' identities.

Alexander demonstrates that power asserted over others can take numerous forms—not just economic or social or political power—but also spiritual power. By holding spiritual power over others, we have the propensity to demean those with whom we disagree by our judgmental or self-righteous behavior. This realization should cause everyone to reflect deeply on how we conduct our lives and the ways in which we may belittle or disparage others. Alexander urges those who have been wounded by the very real oppressions of our society, for instance, not to turn their woundedness into an opportunity to objectify all members of the larger group of people that had previously objectified them. Hurt must not become hate.

By contrast, when we internalize the belief that every human being is created in the image of God, then we can work toward the goal of drawing everyone into an intimate relationship with God and each other. Working on this premise would result in everyone's liberation—a loving approach toward all, including those from whom we have nothing to gain. This will occur only when we "walk in an attitude of repentance," as Alexander puts it. When we recognize our estrangement before God, when we become aware that "Jesus sought me when a stranger, wandering from the fold of God," that awareness of divine acceptance and affirmation opens us up to be able to receive and love any person who may previously have appeared "strange" to us.

The will to power must be challenged—in every human system and in every person—including in the lives of each individual reading this book, so that God's power can be enacted for God's glory and the building up of the reign of God. May it be so.

PREFACE

What causes fights and quarrels among you? Don't they come from your desires that battle within you? Jas 4:1 (NIV)

I wrote this volume over several years out of a deep sense of disappointment at the level of fragmentation and hostility among people who I love dearly but who cannot seem to be able to fully love and live in community with each other. It seeks to accomplish two tasks. First, to help people of faith understand the theological implications of a conception of the Will to Power within its religio-ethical or theo-political framework. It attempts to demonstrate how this phenomenon is played out within the contexts of the various isms –racism, sexism, generationalism, ableism, classism, homo—and heterophobia, nationalism, and economic oppression—that continue to plague contemporary society and threaten human flourishing. Secondly, to suggest theological correctives that might assist in mitigating the deadening effects this malady holds on each member of the global community of individuals who are all loved by God.

The overarching aim of this work is to prompt Christians to intentionally live out the already-but-not-yet dimension of God's Kingdom in a manner that allows more genuinely human and community relationships to unfold. For, I sense within the core of my being that there is a more authentic way—a "more excellent way"[3]—to live out Christian community than is exhibited in the tensions that continually swirl around us. Further, I am hopeful that this work might

---

[3] I Cor 13: 31b

prod us to take seriously the demanding work that such an authentic Christian ethic involves.

To think that such a project would be easy is to live in a delusion. It is to not seriously consider the depth of the debilitating situation in which we find ourselves. To conclude that any solution can be reached fairly quickly would require us to ignore all that has gone before us in getting us to this place.

Yet, to intimate that such a project is too ambitious is to capitulate to the Will to Power, with all its poisonous consequences, as the only feasible option. It is to surrender the possibility of the inbreaking of vestiges of the already-but-not-yet Kingdom within this present world. It is to deny the capacity of the Holy Spirit to create a community where there is "neither Jew nor Greek,... neither slave nor free man,... male nor female; for are all one in Christ Jesus."[4] Moreover, it capitulates to the basest desires of those who fuel the discontent and sense of broken community at the seat of our strained life together.

Though not a work of biblical theology, this project intentionally draws heavily on Scripture as a foundation for centering its propositions and responses. For as a biblical womanist, I find this the safest place from which to attack the variety of disruptive modes of othering that threaten Christian community as well as the flourishing of human relationships.

I have no delusions that this work, or the correctives it suggests, are cure-alls for racial, ethnic, gender, class, theological or other divisions intrinsic to the twenty-first century situation in which we find ourselves as people of faith. I hope, however, it can launch a conversation about how we might come to terms with the realities of these divisions, and through such conversation, might begin to move toward living out a vision of the not yet Kingdom in the here and now.

---

[4]Gal 3:28

INTRODUCTION

"Nation will rise against nation, and kingdom against kingdom." Lk 21:10

The 1992 Rodney King incident in Los Angeles, California was infamous for several reasons. In that episode, four white Los Angeles police officers were acquitted of assault after being video-taped brutalizing King, a black motorist, during an arrest for driving while intoxicated following a high-speed car chase. The entire affair was seen by many in the African America community as a travesty of justice. In the wake of the verdict, several days of rioting and indiscriminate mob violence broke out within the Los Angeles black community as angry, frustrated people of all ages took to the streets to protest what they saw as a vivid playing out of the remnant of racial insensitivity that continues to scar the American spiritual psyche.

The racial implications of the unfolding of these events were overwhelming, highlighting underlying discontent on both sides. Destruction, revenge and retaliation seemed, to some, the only appropriate response to the sense of enormous injustice in what came to be known as "the King verdict." Ironically, that vengeance was not directed toward the four police officers who had mishandled King, or on the department that had hired them. Instead, most of the ensuing violence was lodge against innocent bystanders who happened to be in the wrong place at the wrong time. Moreover, much of the destruction that violence produced occurred within the, already desperate, black community rather among the white power structure that was ostensibly its target. My most vivid recollection of the misplaced vengeance (viewing events from the safe distance of a television screen three thousand miles away) was the scene of a white trucker, Reginald Denny, being pulled from his vehicle and beaten senselessly by a black mob. His only offense was driving through the black neighborhood at the height of the tension

As a seminarian, my interest in social justice caused me to wait to hear the churches' response to these critical moments–the police brutality, the seemingly unfair verdict, and the resulting unrest. I was particularly concerned about how my multi-racial Evangelical denomination would respond. Yet, as in many former cases of national injustice, the silence was deafening—from local pulpits of either black or white pastors, as well as from denominational leaders.

What stood out most as the episode unfolded, however, was a simple question posed by King. Looking into the lens of the news cameras intently focused on him, he intoned wearily, "Can we all get along?" That primitively phrased, seemingly naïve, question-lament summed up why so much hostility exists among various racial, ethnic, cultural, economic or national groups—not just in this nation—but in the world? The still lingering query speaks volumes about the complexity of human relations between men and women, people of differing races, cultures, and classes, as well as those holding divergent theological, political or social positions, or exiting in any category of otherness.

While the question on the lips of a, seemingly, vindicated King appeared to be innocuous, it stands at the heart of the socio-cultural context shaping our modern existence. That question focuses on the, largely unacknowledged, reality that the plethora of isms that have plagued humanity from the beginning or recording time, make it all but impossible to accomplish such a seeming unpretentious task: allowing each other space and permission to flourish fully as unique individuals. It centers on a set of intricate truths about the human condition, and the condition between "Christian" communities as "wars and rumors of wars"[5] continue to circulate around us, and among various groups in our nation, our local communities, and the church.

Defining the Will to Power

As a political theologian, frequently deliberating over this situation, it occurs that from the beginning of Creation, there was never a time when the world was entirely at peace. There has always been some hostile situation or arena somewhere on the globe. It not only occurs between nations, as was the focus of Jesus' discourse. Communities within nations continually conflict with each other as cultural identities, class position, religious affiliation, and other social identifiers place entire groups at war with entire other groups – if not physically, at least philosophically, socially, psychologically, and spiritually.

There are breakdowns in all family structures due to misunderstandings of gender roles, competing generational expectations or plain interpersonal confusion. In the earliest chapters of the Christian canon, the narrative depicts a state of contention in which the first offspring of the first couple found themselves seriously estranged from each other. "Then Cain killed Abel, his brother."[6] From that point, misunderstanding and violence, at some level, have been interwoven into the fabric of interpersonal relationships and continue to be played out in domestic abuse, ever increasing divorce rates and every type of family dysfunction.

Each person, social group, community or nation contends that they are acting ethically and reasonably while the other is not. Each contends that their position is reasonable and honorable while that of the other is not. Each sees their cause as worthy of justice-seeking, as

---

[5] Matt 24:6, Lk 13:7

[6] Gen 4:1-8.

they define justice. Yet, most times, the conflict remains unresolved. Given that the conflict, at its root, is a spiritual contest generated out of a core flaw of the fallen human nature in each of us.

Our lived realities form attitudes that color our interactions with the rest of the world, our individual communities and everyone we encounter. We learn to trust those individuals and groups that are most like us and to distrust those who are different, developing, what philosopher, Rene Girard, defines as, a common sense—a need to protect our group—our family, our community, our tradition's self-interest from the other.[7]

The Will to Power, then, describes this common, innate, drive that is lodged within each man or woman, to understand oneself as being in some way—spiritually, intellectually, ethically, emotionally, physically superior to—or more genuinely human, more reflective of the image of God, and, consequently, more powerful than–at least one other individual. This drive provides us with a justification for our existence. For it assures us, that in the last estimation, we are not totally inferior to everyone else. Since, within this paradigm, every human being participates in this base privation, the divide between personal and structural sinfulness is dissolved. No social structure exists without individuals that make singular and collective decisions immediately implicating their entire group, as well as having mediated implications for those outside their sphere. There are no individual acts outside of an existing social reality—or set or realities. Moreover, those realities influence attitudes and actions sometimes in blatantly observable ways, but often in an imperceptible—or unacknowledged—manner. We are all, to some degree and in some form, guilty of the Will to Power, and this privation does not depend on whether we wield substantial material power over the other.

We participate in the Will to Power whenever we employ the terms "those people" "them" or they" to describe (as individuals or

---

[7] Rene Girard, *Violence and the Sacred*. Baltimore: Johns Hopkins University Press, 1977.

collectively) an entire other race, culture, gender, or class of people made up of persons possessing individual egos, aspirations, and levels of spiritual, social, cultural and intellectual development. When we use the terms "people like us, or the collective "we" to privilege the position of our group, we operate in the Will to Power. For, at the same time, we are dismissing some other individuals as, somehow, not deserving the same level of respect, dignity, attention or benefit as those whom we consider like ourselves. However, no other individual is completely like us; each is the other is some way. So ultimately, no other person entirely escapes the working out of the Will to Power in their relationship to us.

This tendency toward the Will to Power provides the dynamic fuel for all isms: racism, sexism, misogyny, ageism, nationalism, culturalism, ableism, and the numerous phobias we hold about people of other social, spiritual or cultural identities. Moreover, the spiritual blindness that is a flaw of our fallenness often allows us to quickly discern the tendency toward Will to Power in colleagues and collaborators without being able to detect it in ourselves. Or, more often, we sense that our strand of the malady is less harmful than that exhibited by others. Yet, no one completely escapes its tentacles and any abatement of its grasp is achieved only with intense self-reflection and discipline. And even then, it lodges just below the surface of our spiritual skin, waiting for the opportune moment to reassert itself.

Again, all of us succumb to the Will to Power at some time, in one or more ways. This tendency makes it difficult to authentically embrace any other person in full, agape Christian love, even those to whom we consider ourselves close—family members, friends, colleagues, and fellow believers. For, we assume that, surely, no other person is quite as authentic as we are. The unfortunate end of this attitude is that the kind of intimate relationality for which each of us was created is never entirely apprehended. This innate Will to Power leaves each of us—flawed as we are by our sinful nature—a little less complete than our Maker intended. And this deficiency in our finite understanding hides the reality of our own complicity in the continuing reign of the Will to Power within us.

Yet, while the Will to Power is innate in every human being, the way in which its internal form finds external expression in attitudes and actions depends on several factors: It, first, is shaped by the cultural milieu in which we have been formed and nurtured. For embedded within that culture are unfortunate ways of thinking about those who stand outside of it. These assumptions are held, embellished, cherished, and passed down through generations of folklore, ways of interacting, and even spiritual justification. Often, without being aware of what we are doing or questioning their validity, we take them on, internalize them and begin to live them out. In many cases, these ideas are never tested by any authentic engagement with members of the subject groups. Solely, then, on the strength of our trust in the community's wisdom, we take on aspects of the Will to Power.

And these assumptions continue to be woven into the fabric of the expression of the Will to Power in us. The implantation and imbibing of cultural determinants are often imperceptible as they happen in ever more subtle ways and, indeed, are part of the fabric of our particular cultural milieu. In our daily discourses, cues are provided for how the other should be treated. Which others are to be considered friends? Which are to be respected? Which are to be feared? Suggestions are made about which others it is safe to approach, and which are to be avoided—or eliminated—at all costs.

Further, in part, the specific shape the Will to Power takes in each of us is formed by whether our context is considered dominant or subordinate and by our position within its pecking order. Those who are part of the dominant culture feel safe in openly expressing this Will to Power, for their assumptions are supported by the outworking of the system. Almost everything around them tells them they are right about the other. Laws are shaped to favor them, cultural norms are established in their interest, "official" findings of dominant institutions bolster arguments, attitudes, and opinions expressed in public media undergird long-held suppositions and further shape embedded assumptions.

Those within the subordinate culture find more clandestine and subversive expressions of the Will to Power. Much time and effort are spent circumventing systems that are considered oppressive. And, those who, seemingly, lack power congratulate themselves for their superior cunning in being able to outwit more powerful individuals and systems. In the end, this subterfuge, too, is an expression of the Will to Power

Yet, ultimately, the Will to Power finds concrete expression in some form in every individual, community, culture or nation. For it is the inevitable outworking of the ubiquitous innate condition. No one is immune to it—or innocent of it.

For, to us, no one is entirely our equal. Yet, neither is anyone, simply, different from us or, from our way of seeing the world. Each of the other is experienced as either superior or inferior to us in some manner. They are sensed as, in one way or another, more—or less—human than we are. They appear as more—or less—deserving of respect than ourselves. And, consequently, we innately, often without thinking about it, respond to that sense of position in ways that surprise even us.

Though slavery and much of legal Jim Crowism has been abolished for decades, for example, some members of minority communities respond to those within the dominant culture with a deferent posture, while at the same time, inwardly distrusting, or even loathing, them. Conversely, some within the dominant culture, find it difficult to completely dismantle the stereotypes embedded in our psyches as the natural consequence of decades of incredibly harsh mistreatment.

If we deem that the other is superior, we must master them in some existential manner. We must become as good or better than they are to diffuse their perceived power over us. For, we sense that they can never be completely depended on to protect or promote our interest. We think that they will, continually, find ways to take advantage of us or use us to their advantage. Many, black people, for example, generally distrust the motivation of, even sympathetic, white liberals as being ingenuine. They sense that white colleagues—no matter how earnest they appear or helpful they might have been—will sooner or later, reveal their true motivation. They insist that blacks who completely trust any white person is either naïve, misguided, or is a sellout.

When we consider the other inferior in any manner, we can seemingly be gracious, but we must, always, in some way, keep them at arm's length. We must ensure that they stay in their proper place. Further, we sense that we can never fully disclose ourselves to them or allow them to disclose themselves fully to us. For, to do this, would create a false sense of intimacy and draw us too tightly into a false sense of relationship. More importantly, it would take away any advantage, we seemingly, or actually, have over them.

In either case, we sense that keeping them at arms-length, ensures they cannot contaminate us or bring us down to their level. So, we can never become completely comfortable with them. For, we must continue to be on top of the situation, so they cannot rob us of what we deserve. We are always aware that to give to them is, ultimately, to take from us. If they are to gain, in the end, we must, somehow, lose.

Those who are a part of Western culture, for instance, count it as superior—more advanced and more Christian—than Eastern culture. Men consider themselves ontologically more reflective of the image of God than women. And, though race is a social construct, and no one has a pure racial identity, the group that identifies itself as white is considered by some of its members genetically superior to all other races.

We take on whatever form of the Will to Power most common to us; most convenient, most comfortable, and importantly, most easily hidden from us – and others. Or, we assume the form that nets us the most material or psychic capital. We rationalize our assumption by telling ourselves that, in some way, it is *their* fault that they are not like or equal to us. If *they* would fall in line, if they would reform *themselves* either up or down to our level, we could all do as King suggested and get along. But, we tell ourselves that because of their inherent deficiency, such equality is not possible.

The Will to Power assumes endless forms. White women can feel superior to black women. Black men can feel superior to black women. Wealthy people can feel economically superior to the less wealthy; while working class and poor people can feel spiritually superior to the wealthy. Christians or Moslems can feel superior to those who hold other beliefs. And those who are religious in any form feel superior to all who are not, who conversely feel superior to superstitious religious folk.

Rationalizing the Will to Power

For the Will to Power to make sense to us, we must justify our innate inability to accept the other as equal. We must tell ourselves the big lie and convince ourselves that, "we are this way in relation to them, because they make us this way." It is the only way we can maintain our stance and our place and still maintain any sense of integrity. After all, we are strong, we are pure, we are Christian, we are civilized, we are educated or enlightened—and the list goes on. We do not hold irrational ideas about other people or the world they live in—those other people are irrational. It gets formulated in diverse ways, but it is the same lie. It is their fault, the whole group of them, that we do not engage them. They are just not like us.

Some white people do not like black people (as a group), for example, because they are held to be uncouth, lazy, less intelligent, and more inclined to moral failure. For some white people, it is even easier to see black people, or Asian people or Latino people as a separate, lower class of human being, unable to attain the same intellectual and spiritual capacity as themselves. American slave masters, for example, told themselves that their black slaves, were only three-fifths of a human being,[8] did not have the same type of soul as themselves and white colleagues, and certainly could not attain the same level of redemption. Further, they told themselves, that should they chance to receive redemption, these ontologically inferior people could not possibly be expected to occupy the same quarters of heaven as themselves.

Yet, despite popular contentions to the contrary, racism on the part of blacks is equally as rampant. Many black people do not like white people as a group and consider all white people racist. Notwithstanding the genuine historical pattern of bitter racial disparity that has existed for centuries in the United States and globally, they mentally negate any subsequent strides that individual members of the white community have made to live out justice in relation to other races, and discount these efforts is ingenuine.

The misfortune is that no degree of transformation or conciliation has been enough to dislodge the seed of bitterness implanted by the horrors of, undeniably, one of the worse chapters in human history. For some black people, white people are innately evil or morally defective. For those who hold this attitude, white people are inheritors of a legacy of oppression and, as a group, should be feared or, at least, distrusted. Those who hold this mindset operate on underlying ideas of reverse prejudice not easily erased by the sincerest overtures from the white community. No attempt by any white person to accept them as equal or offer reconciliation is taken seriously. For, they assume that no white person is ever truly an intimate friend, and they are always somewhat suspicious that all white people secretly regard all black

---

8 The legalized form of this assertion was codified in the 1787 compromise between the southern and northern United States that established that for tax purposes and determining legislative representation, each slave would be counted as three-fifths of a person toward determining the total population of a state.

people as less than themselves. The dominant narrative for this group is that all white people possess a sense of entitlement; for, after all, almost all the real power within society is held by them and, in many instances, has been used to the detriment of others. This line of reasoning makes all white people, as a group, morally deficient and, therefore, spiritually inferior to black people.

The same pattern, often, holds within gendered relationships. Some men disregard, disrespect, or mistreat women out of a sense that women must be kept in their place. The suggestion is that those women who are not, in some way, weak or silly, are manipulative and dangerous. The myth of female inferiority has been handed down through generations and exists in almost every culture and context. This gendered Will to Power colors almost every aspect of interaction between the sexes—interpersonal, family, workplace and community relationships, as well as those within communities of faith.

Unfortunately, within the Christian context, such attitudes on gender, race and even class may be given biblical warrant. Proof texts, especially from the Pauline corpus, are purported to uphold a plethora of isms, most notably, the justification of slavery, and the subjugation of women in the church and home.

Paul's admonition for slaves to obey [their] masters[9] allowed American slave owners to feel at ease in justifying generations of oppression. For those bent on keeping women "in their place," the coupling of the Genesis narrative of the deception of Eve by the serpent with the Pauline texts "requiring" subordination is, apparently, adequate proof of God's stamp of approval on the position in which men often place women:

[9]Eph 6:5-9

To the woman [God] said, I will make your pains in childbearing very severe; with painful labor, you will give birth to children. Your desire will be for your husband, and he will rule over you.[10]

For the man is not of the woman; but the woman of the man. Neither was the man created for the woman; but the woman for the man."[11]

And Adam was not the one deceived; it was the woman who was deceived and, first, became a sinner.[12]

Christian patriarchy underlaid a 500-year enthusiasm for witch-burning that resulted in the torture and murder of as many as 1,000,000 women and girls. In non-Christian societies, fundamentalist interpretations of religious texts of every sort have been used to justify both racist and misogynist attitudes and behavior of every ilk. This type of hermeneutic has produced and justified every kind of carnage: genocide, rape, the kidnapping and enslavement of wives, the exposure of female infants, and the human sacrifice of virgin girls.

In the more broadly religious sphere, Christians convince themselves, that they are more deserving of God's grace (though totally *unmerited,* by definition) than are people of other faith traditions. For these Christians, while God so loves the world, yet God loves Christians more, and is more concerned about their, temporal and eternal, wellbeing than that of other groups. Entire theologies are derived, promoted, learned and internalized to support this proposition. In extreme cases, we are not at all sure that these people are worthy of God's salvific project—that they can attain to the salvation God freely offers to all of humankind.

---

[10]Gen 3:16

[11]I Cor 11:8-9

[12]I Tim 2:14

Having convinced ourselves that God does not love them in the same way, or to the same degree, that God loves us, we are satisfied with the contention that we are not obligated to show these fellow human beings, who have been created equally in God's image, with any degree of civility or respect. We tell ourselves that, at the least, it is enough to disregard them entirely; or at the extreme, that all of them are plotting our demise, and must be avoided at all costs. And we stand, therefore, perpetually, at odds with each other, to the point of war.

The Concept of Will to Power in Nietzsche

I did not come to my concept of the Will to Power on my own; but adapted it from the term developed by nineteenth century philosopher, Friedrich Nietzsche. His application of the concept runs counter to my own assessment, so it might seem bold to adopt terminology that has gained a great measure of capital in this different context. Yet, no other term so aptly describes the situation of our contemporary society. Whether we verbalize it, we each see our group as the norm—the high point and the supreme expression – of the human family. We believe in our own superiority. Specifically, Nietzsche advanced the bold proposition that,

> . . .every specific body strives to become master over all space and to extend its force (its will to power) and to thrust back all that resists its extension. But it continually encounters similar efforts on the part of other bodies and ends by coming to an arrangement ("union") with those of them that are sufficiently related to it; thus, they then conspire together for power.[13]

---

[13] Frederick Nietzsche *The Will to Power,* Section 636, Walter Kaufmann and R. J. Hollingdale, translators. New York: Vintage Press, 345.

Nietzsche saw every living being as reflecting the Will to Power—striving to seize and become predominant. For him, this is the only way to preserve life, which itself is Will to Power.[14] Though he concedes there are "unpleasant" features—a will to dominate, rule, control, and force one's will upon others, he contends they are necessary for our survival. For him, "exploitation" is an essential part of whatever lives. As a basic organic function; it is the very will to life and humankind or civilization could not survive without it. [15]

Nietzsche understood life itself as essentially overpowering and suppressing whatever is alien and weaker, imposing our own mold on them, and exploiting them for what they provide us.[16] Yet he did not see those who exploit as corrupt.[17] For him, such exploitation is a necessity of life.[18]

Nietzsche's conception ratifies the social Darwinist notion of "the survival of the fittest." He equated strength with nobility and decried what he saw as an unfortunate revaluation of "noble" values. For unlike Darwin, he saw the strong (the noble) ultimately losing the battle for survival against the weak, whom he saw as manifesting the opposite will to nothingness—nihilism.[19]

Nietzsche held that such qualities as hardness, forcefulness, slavery, and tyranny enhanced the human species as much as stoicism and experimentation and much more than their opposites grace and agape love.[20] He believed that the Will to Power benefits humanity more than altruism or kindness, as the foundation of human flourishing.

---

[14] Frederick Nietzsche. *Beyond Good and Evil,* 13, 259.

[15] Ibid., 226

[16] Ibid., 258.

[17] Ibid.

[18] Ibid., 259; See also, Frederick Nietzsche, *On the Genealogy of Morals: A Polemic,* 2:11; 3:7.

[19] Ibid., 2:24

[20] *Beyond Good and Evil* 44

For Nietzsche, the only credible option is to dominate something – or someone. For he saw the failure to do so as being perpetually controlled, channeled, contained, or negated by the other. For him, higher cultures are derived from strong cultures pitting themselves against weaker, more civilized, more peaceful races.[21] Ultimately, Nietzsche saw those who exhibited it, through the strength of soul, as more wholly human.[22]

Nietzsche was not unaware that the simple Will to Power could become unmanageable when the pleasure of the sense of power and the hunger to continue to overpower – though already on top – supersedes it. Though he understood that unharnessed Will to Power does not stop once it has attained a position of total supremacy, his positive assessment does not align with Christian anthropology or soteriology in seriously considering the depth of human sinfulness. The fallen nature continually lusts for more authority and can never be satiated until it reaches that point of supremacy.

Yet, neither does it reflect deeply enough on the possibility of genuine repentance and redemption. His appraisal assumes that the unredeemed, fallen condition is the only possible state, and that Christian faith's attempt to show, "a more excellent way,"[23] is out of step with reality. Assessments such as his are what make reconciliation so difficult. They keep us from attaining the level of human relationship for which we were created. Yet, they do not provide a rationale for abandoning the project.

---

[21] Ibid., 201.

[22] Ibid., 257

[23] I Cor 12:31b

GOD IN OUR IMAGE

God created humankind in God's own image, in the image of God
He created humankind; male and female God created them. Gen 1:27

A central claim of Christian anthropology is that humankind is uniquely unlike the rest of the created order and are the only earthly beings that are capable of fully signifying the nature of God. What makes us human, is that we – and no other member of the created order – are crafted by our Creator as a reflection of God's self. We were fashioned as God's representatives on the earth.

We were not created as little gods, for as created beings, all our powers are derived. We can create nothing of ourselves or for ourselves. The dominion we are to exercise over the rest of creation has been vested in us by our Creator and we have no claim to any inherent power. Still, we are the only component of God's creation that shares in God's communicable attributes—goodness, justice, rationality, and wisdom—though to a much lesser degree.

Still, Christian anthropology further asserts that, as part of that created order, humankind shares in the finitude of the rest of creation. Not owning God's incommunicable attributes, we exist within the limits of time, space, and the capacity for understanding our individual selves and our world.

Through the Fall, each of us shares in the further limitation imposed by sin. Accordingly, we bear two distinct, opposing realities in our nature. Each of us, severally and together, carry within ourselves the possibility of a degree of transcendence or growth toward spiritual flourishing. Yet, we also carry within us the weight of a despicable fallen nature that is susceptible to further spiritual decline. We are at the same time capable of great achievement and of great depravity; the tension this poses within us leading to an ongoing battle to allow the better element to have control.

The Christian tradition contends that through specific revelation, the eternal Creator of the universe unveiled the essence of God's character to us. We argue that the disclosure given through God's activity with Israel and the church, God's inscripturated and proclaimed Word, and the Incarnation of the Son who dwelt among us, exceeds any knowledge available through human senses, the natural sciences or other religions. We are persuaded that this revelation is true and sure and that we have gotten it right.

Despite God's gracious unveiling of God's self, however, God is exponentially greater than any separate element of Creation, or of all of Creation, collectively. What we have apprehended of God only approximates who the eternal, omnipotent, omniscient, omnipresent One is. For, a major limitation of our finitude is our inability to discern the entire reality of who God is. We cannot comprehend God's vastness or the totality of all that is included in God's being. Anselm's ontological argument that God is "a being than which none greater can be conceived,"[24] does not adequately capture the fullness of God's infinite reality that is far beyond anything we might even, reasonably, try to understand.

Yet, in our hubris, we are prone to presume that since we are made in, and reflect, God's image, God must be like *us*. God must reflect what we have determined are our individual virtues, merits, and

---

[24] Anselm, St., *Anselm's Basic Writings,* translated by S.W. Deane, 2nd Ed. La Salle, IL: Open Court Publishing Co., 1962.

strengths—only in greater abundance. God must have our aptitude for relationship but at a more intimate level and share our intellectual acuity, but to a much sharper degree. God must love the things we love—beauty, goodness, integrity—as *we* define them, but in super abundance.

More importantly, our corollary understanding is more problematic in that we not only suppose that God is like *us*, but that God, assuredly, is unlike *them*. It is not that God is only partially like them or less like them and more like us. In our estimation of ultimate reality, God is so exponentially removed from being like them that God is the absolute opposite of what and who they are.

As we image God, God has our likes and dislikes. In fact, God not only loves what we love, but God hates what we hate. Not just us as individuals, but our entire culture—our ethical, moral, spiritual and aesthetic values represent the highest level attainable by a non-deity. These values approximate the closest to the re-creation of paradise or the Kingdom of God. We have convinced ourselves that all other representations pale in comparison.

Such ideations are both idolatrous and narcissistic. Idolatrous in that whatever state we find ourselves, we try to remake God in that image. Though God revealed Godself as Spirit—having no human physical or cultural form, we continue to claim that the fullest manifestation of that Spirit is represented in the highest elements of our community.

Various iterations of theology are brazened in insisting on this point. If we are black, then God is black.[25] Or white, brown, red, or yellow. God must epitomize all that it means to be us or how could God be for us. How could God assist us in our project of self-

---

[25] See, for example, James Cone, *A Black Theology of Liberation*. Philadelphia: J.B. Lippincott (1970, 14-16. Though Cone nuances this assertion to posit a God who is on the side of all oppressed people, he certainly rejects a homogenized conception of a God who is equally concerned about the oppressor.

deification? And though this idea is seldom coherently articulated, the dominant Western culture assumes that God is a white male with Western cultural sensitivities, and certainly, not like the "primitives" who represent other cultures.

If we are women, then God must be a woman. Yet, while Christian Scripture contends that God made both female and male in God's image, denoting that God has a *feminine* side, not all of God is feminine. Neither do God's feminine attributes negate God's masculine qualities.[26] God exhibits both strength and nurture in both fathering and mothering; showing strong discipline and undying love at the same time. To cast God as entirely feminine or masculine as a way of claiming any spiritual or moral privilege entirely misses the point. We are all—male and female—created in God's indelible image. As a part of the God-imaged creation, we all—male and female of every race and culture—share equally in God's project of inclusive Kingdom relationship. As we understand this, we can visualize God in a manner that resonates with our own human situatedness without recreating God in our own image or devaluing the refection of that image within the other.

William Young's contemporary Christian fiction, *The Shack*,[27] depicts the first person of the Trinity as a character named Papa—a bosomy black woman with dreadlocks who is as much at home in the kitchen as in any other realm of the universe. From her unique vantage point, Papa dispenses wisdom to anyone who will visit. When a friend informed me that I would not be able to put the book down, I was underwhelmed. But as I read, I was intrigued that a middle-aged white guy presented a portrait—an image of God—that incorporated the essence, at least on the surface, of who I, as an African American woman, appear to be.

---

[26] Those qualities implied in these terms are difficult to define and are certainly culturally loaded.

[27] Young, William P. *The Shack: Where Tragedy Confronts Eternity.* Newbury Park, CA: Windblown Media, 2007.

I was enthralled by that image of God I had never encountered. For the first time, I was presented with a depiction of my Creator that, in no way, negated me and it was inviting. This portrait repudiated other depictions of God that had been forced on me through years in the church, as well as vindicated my aspirations to be fully reflected in God. It was tempting to linger in that imagery; to embrace it as the truest possible depiction of God that had been missed by theologians through the centuries. What made the temptation more tenable was that the two other persons depicted as part of the Godhead were a Hispanic man and an Asian woman—a sort of multi-cultural, equal opportunity Godhead. Yet, as soothing, comforting and embraceable as that depiction is, to hold onto it would be idolatrous. To privilege that image assumes that all that is important about God is wrapped up in such a characterization. It requires me to buy into the idolatry that I decry in other depictions.

We too easily excuse ourselves from the temptation to idolatry. For, after all, we tell ourselves, as the victimized we deserve to be vindicated by a God who prioritizes our liberation. If we are poor, then we imagine a God who is poor and offers to us a "preferential option."[28] God must be opposed to all those who are rich, no matter how legitimately they obtained their wealth or generously they share those riches. Else, how could God be touched by our infirmities? How else could he be in solidarity with us?

Yet, this preferential option cannot, rightfully, be understood as the exclusion of all the rest of humanity. Scripture is clear, that God has a heart for the poor and that God expects those who embrace faith to share that heart. Surely, the prophets, as well as the life and ministry of Jesus, clearly indict those who mistreat the poor. Yet God does not disdain those who are rich in material goods based, solely, on the possessions they hold.

The breadth of God's wealth is undeniable, and God desires to share that wealth with all of Creation. God is not only the Creator of

---

[28]See, for example, Gustavo Gutierrez, *A Theology of Liberation: History, Politics, and Salvation*. Maryknoll, NY: Orbis Books, 1988.

everything that was made; God owns it all. God has no lack of resources. God's love for the poor, then, is not a denial of God's love for the rich or the powerful. God's eternal yearning is to be in communion with all of Creation regardless of the individual's material stature. For we are all poor in spirit, lacking the spiritual fortitude to save ourselves or provide for our ultimate requirements. We are all equally in need of a savior. All are captive to the same innate human longings that can only be satisfied with that which is truly spiritual.

God does not paint all of those who are rich with a broad stroke that indicts them for simply having material assets. And according to Christian Scripture, God promises the blessing of abundant material possessions to those who are faithful.[29] Further, God must be given credit for giving individuals, as members of His family, the ability and resources to accumulate wealth. For clearly, simple material gain is not the problem. Rather, God sanctions those who gain from the exploitation of those powerless to defend themselves. Christian Scripture, specifically, denounces personal or institutional gain that comes at the expense of those who are already dispossessed.[30] Further, it denounces gain that is squandered on the selfish pursuit of hedonistic excess.[31]

If we are middle class, we are convinced that God must be a God of moderation – neither desperately poor nor interested in vast material gain. The values of solid middle-class existence, (hard work, respectability, communal harmony) must be God's values. It only seems reasonable, for God is, after all, a God of balance. And for many, this balance is best exemplified in a *respectable*, solid, middle-class lifestyle.

If we are extremely successful, then God is that too. For God rules over all the universe. God reigns over every other aspect of Creation and expects the highest element of Creation to be able to do so. Our

---

29 See for example, Deut 28:3-5, Ps 1

30 See for example, Ezek 22:12, Jer 8:10, Amos 8:4-7 and Mic 2:1-3

31 See for example, Prov 21:20

definition of success (prosperity) then becomes God's definition. Our measure of attainment God's measure.

If we are wealthy, then so is God. God must be exuberantly rich and full of material abundance. How else could he provide for all the needs of God's Creation? For us then, a God who is materially poor is an oxymoron, and further is of no use to us. Yet, even a God who would identify himself with the materially poor is useless. For what benefit could such a God be. Such a God has nothing to contribute to our wellbeing.

If we are white, God must be white, and because of His ontological nature, God has designed a divine social order that puts whites at the top to keep everyone else in line. For to us, whiteness denotes more than skin color. It carries with it the required moral and intellectual capacity to do what is necessary to maintain that order and prevent chaos.

More specifically, if we are white males, God must be a white male, and has further stratified the social order to keep women in line as well. God chose the superior creature, endowed with the intellectual, and spiritual acumen that is most like God, to paternalistically provide for the protection of all others. Since, like God, we know what is best for all others, we have the faculties to establish and maintain protective systems that allow benefits of the established order to "trickle down."

For no matter what our position, we seek to export—or impose—our idea of the fullest representation of God to all others. And we are vexed when they cannot see this as the most reflective image of God or cannot align themselves with that reflection. So, we move further away from the other to keep from marring the image we seek to reflect and impose. God must be like us, and, again, not like the other. Or else, how could God be *our* God? Moreover, of what good would God be to *us*? How else could God assist us in our project of self-preservation?

Opposed to this reasoning, the Paul contends that we see "through a glass darkly.[32] With spiritual vision encumbered by a distorted finitude that colors and dims our imprecise vision, we are like the blind men depicted in the poem, "The Blind Men and the Elephant."[33]

It was six men of Hindustan
To learning much inclined,
Who went to see the Elephant
(Though all of them were blind),
That each by observation
Might satisfy his mind

The First approached the Elephant,
And happening to fall
Against his broad and sturdy side,
At once began to bawl:
"God bless me! but the Elephant
Is very like a wall!"

The Second, feeling of the tusk,
Cried, "Ho! what have we here
So very round and smooth and sharp?
To me 'tis mighty clear
This wonder of an Elephant
Is very like a spear!"

The Third approached the animal,
And happening to take
The squirming trunk within his hands,

---

[32] 1 Cor 13:12

[33] John Godfrey Saxe "The Blind Men and the Elephant" in *The Poems of John Godfrey Saxe* (Highgate Edition), Boston: Houghton, Mifflin and Company, 1881.

Thus boldly up and spake:
"I see," quoth he, "the Elephant
Is very like a snake!"

The Fourth reached out an eager hand,
And felt about the knee.
"What most this wondrous beast is like
Is mighty plain," quoth he;
"'Tis clear enough the Elephant
Is very like a tree!"

The Fifth, who chanced to touch the ear,
Said: "E'en the blindest man
Can tell what this resembles most;
Deny the fact who can
This marvel of an Elephant
Is very like a fan!"

The Sixth no sooner had begun
About the beast to grope,
Than, seizing on the swinging tail
That fell within his scope,
"I see," quoth he, "the Elephant
Is very like a rope!"

And so these men of Indostan
Disputed loud and long,
Each in his own opinion
Exceeding stiff and strong,
Though each was partly in the right,
And all were in the wrong!

So oft in theologic wars,
The disputants, I ween,
Rail on in utter ignorance

Of what each other mean,
And prate about an Elephant
Not one of them has seen!

Whatever part of God we can apprehend from our limited cultural, social, or theological vantage point, we surmise must be all of God. Moreover, to us, it is absurd for anyone to suggest otherwise. For after all, if they could stand where we stand, they could surely see God more clearly.

Through the language of another era, the message is relevant to our postmodern reality. We, like these men, discern as much of God as our fallen senses, constricted by the prejudice of our context as well by our innate sinfulness, can appropriate. Yet, from this hugely restricted vantage point, we are satisfied with what we sense and, mistakenly, convince that thus can be all of that there is of God.

It is not only Christian faith that we deem reflects truth, but our brand of that faith. The narrowness of much of Christian theology is epitomized in Saxe's poem. We see the part of God—the part of the Body of Christ that we touch—or more precisely, that touches us, as the whole reality of God's design for the church and the Kingdom. In our spiritually near-sighted fallibility, we fail to recognize it as only part and claim that the part of God's revelation to which we have been privileged is the entirety of revelation, to the exclusion of all else.

Yet, again, the Apostle's contention of the darkened view through the glass highlights our problem. Since *our* perception of Ultimate Reality is its entirety for us, we leave no room for the other to contribute to our understanding. In our assessment, all other iterations of faith are flawed and need the clarification that only our tradition can bring. Instead of a slice that helps make up the loaf, *our* tradition – our theological system becomes the whole loaf for us.

With this stance, God is no longer mystery to us. For, in our minds, we have solved God's inscrutability by ascribing supreme worth only to One who is just like us. We, justify our actions and attitudes toward the other by seeing them as the same and attitudes that any true God would hold. God's perceived hatred of our enemies is justification enough for our attempt to destroy them. God's distaste for their inadequate or inappropriate reading of the faith is adequate reason for our violent denunciation of them. We allow no room for a middle ground position, mediation or reconciliation. We have seen God's enemy and it is them!

In invoking this position, we continually deify ourselves while vilifying the other—simply because they are other. We cannot—or have not attempted to—understand them. And since we do not understand them, they cannot be like God. Since we do not understand them, we come to fear them. And since we fear them, we must, psychically and spiritually, destroy them or at least vilify them. For we sense that if we do not get to them first, they will destroy us, or at least destroy our contention that we are most like God. In taking this stance, we further negate the possibility of a middle position, a shared ground on which all of humankind can cast itself in its common finitude

Authentic humanity is only possible when we refuse to define ourselves, and our God-imaged createdness as over and against the other. Such humanity comes into full focus as we understand that the fullness of God can only be reflected in a common stand with the rest of the human family. All that we know of God is what God has chosen to self-disclose; all that we can say about God is by analogy. Yet, God remains incomprehensible and irreducible to any single characterization we might conjure. Since the perichoretic nature of God lies within interdependent relationship within God's self, God's image is only incompletely reflected in any separation between individuals or communities. That image is never fully reflected when members of the human family stand opposed to each other. To break the intimate fellowship for which we were created is to fracture the best representation of the image of God. It is to render it distorted in its apprehension by the other.

The Hebrew Scripture's injunction against making graven images[34] was not only because of the possibility of worshipping other gods than Yahweh. It also spoke of the reality that any finite conception of God reduces the Creator of the universe to a caricature of the worshipper framed within the limitations of his or her fixed understanding. Such a rendition has dire consequences. And, given we come to see that God is like us, we come to assume that only we speak for God. We assume that we, alone, know God's language. From that, we insist that we are the least likely to mishear or misrepresent God who speaks to us not only about ourselves, but also about them.

The injunction against graven images is one reminder that, in and of ourselves, we are inadequate to the task of representing the mystery of God. None of us have inherent merit above that of another. Any righteousness in us is imputed, and we can claim no credit for it.

God's revelation is true. Yet, because we are locked within our flawed, finite reality, our appropriation of that revelation is always problematic and limited. Most likely, that appropriation benefits us in some way that discriminates against the other. Jesus Christ was the only human being without sin, without finitude, without a flawed perception of himself or his Father. As Christians, if any of us knows God, the Father at all, we know Him most fully through his son, Jesus. Yet, we must always confess that even our knowledge of Jesus is limited by our sinfulness, though it is the only knowledge of Jesus to which we can lay claim.

The greatest reflection of God is the incarnate Christ, not in his cultural or ethnic identity, nor in his gender, but spiritually. Jesus—and only Jesus—among all of humankind reflected every attribute of his Father in full measure. Even that claim must not be heard as an occasion for a bigoted claim for our superiority as Christians. For if we are to be faithful in carrying out God's Kingdom priorities, we are forced to take seriously the reality that Jesus, himself, came into the

---

34 Ex 20:4

world to serve. To claim any solidarity with Jesus through faith, then, we must see ourselves as called to serve the world God so loved; to see ourselves through servant's eyes.

God's attribute of love can be seen by others only when those claiming kinship with Christ are loving as Christ loved. God's attribute of wisdom is displayed only when we use our intellect to benefit all of creation. God's attribute of power—omnipotence—is best comprehended when all our senses—all our limited faculties—are employed to benefit God's world. It is only when we are willing to give ourselves in service to that world, and to die to selfish or narrow ambitions, that we truly reflect God's image.

We, individually and collectively, are a lesser image of God. Alternately, God is a greater—the greatest—image from which any individual or group or all of humankind is drawn. For God is not just a reflection of the best human elements. God possesses communicable attributes that exceed the fullest compilation of all that is found in us.

No, individual or community, then, can claim the sole or purest reflection of God's image. To try to do so is, again, idolatry. Such a claim belies our efforts to grave a lessor image of God in our psyche and spirit. Indeed, God's indelible image can only fully be seen in the collective fellowship of men and women, from every ethnicity and degree of ableness who, as the human community, encompass the world that God so loved.

That image, forged at conception, is made clear through the Spirit's sanctifying empowerment so that the explicit likeness can be made visible in us. For only God's Spirit can burn in our hearts to filter out the dross of ambition, pride, and base self-interest—the Will to Power – that so easily contaminates its clear expression. That image is only fully discerned in unbroken relationship with the other. Recognizing the breach our sinfulness fosters makes it evidence such a degree of relational intimacy is unsustainable without God's help.

We cannot confuse the essential elements of reflection. God does not reflect us. We are to reflect God. For if God's love reflects our love, it is a limited love based on merit and is granted only to those who look like us and act as we expect them to. It is temperamental and meted out with partiality depending on some whim or accident of birth. It is subject to some test of loyalty, or, at least obedience. Further, it is subject to being aborted or short-circuited when a perceived impediment is in place.

If our love reflects God's love it must be active and unconditional. Such love must embrace all of God's Creation. It cannot be deterred by isms that so easily arise within us. It cannot stop at difference. This love, as the Apostle admonishes, is patient, kind, hopes for the good, thinks no evil of the other and never fails. It is a hard pattern to follow and takes a measure of Christian maturity as Paul alludes to in the passage.

If God's mercy reflects our mercy, it is restricted and dependent on perceived merit for which none of us can be entirely deserving. It can be metered out by degree based on our affinity for, or disdain of, the other. It is completely subjective and subject to the whim of the one who dispenses it. It is extended to those who have the moral fortitude to request it, and who we sense will not continually misuse it.

Rather, if our mercy reflects God's mercy, its favor is extended where it is most unmerited and, often, unwelcomed. It is limitless, abundantly generous, and extended to those who least deserve it—to those who have offered the greatest offense, such that as hymnist Fanny Crosby declared, the "vilest offender" has the possibility of receiving our pardon.[35]

God's authentic image is not gendered, nor ethnically, culturally, or economically situated. That image does not reflect the class distinctions of our respective cultures. Neither is it founded on religious sensibilities. It resides equally in all of humankind. The

---

[35] Fannie Crosby, "To God Be the Glory" in Robert Lowry and William Howard Doane, eds., *Brightest and Best: A Choice Collection of New Songs, Duet, Choruses, Invocation and Benediction Hymns for the Sunday School and Meetings of Prayer and Praise.* New York: Biglow & Main, 1875.

redeemed and unredeemed. The saint and the sinner. The good, the bad, and the ugly. For, again, that image is impressed indelibly on each of us at our conception—before we have any opportunity to garner merit or proffer reciprocity.

While our best representations of that image are limited and flawed, it is mirrored in the illustration of a mother's natural love extended to her baby before the moment of birth—before there is any indication of what that child will become. During the gestation period, the mother lathers affection on the child, speaking and singing to the baby while he or she is in the womb. She listens to the heartbeat and feels the movement and she is overjoyed. Once the child enters the world, this complete love continues unabated despite the unpredictability of that child's future or the vicissitudes of that child's life. It is not dependent on the achievement of high status in life and remains secure even if the child becomes what might be considered a horrible failure.

Whether that child is obedient and compliant, or is wayward and rebellious, that mother's love does not end or abate. As far as is humanly possible, that love is unconditional and is one of the closest representations of the caliber of the love God offers to us. But that love is only extended in that way to that child or those children (if there are siblings). No one else outside of that circle can expect to partake of it.

Conversely, all of God's children—every single person conceived or born into the world is offered full participation in God's love and is a full partaker of God's image. Collectively then, we reflect the spitting image of the Father. Separated into our isms, however, we can only hope to reflect a distorted, confusing portrait of the reality of God.

As Christians, who are continually tempted to harness God within our camp, we fail to concede that before the Incarnation, before there was a Christian faith or church, God was interested in all of humankind as God's chief creation. In the limited estimation this failure evidences, when we claim that Christians, ontologically, bear out the image of God more fully than any other group, we deny that the image is indelibly stamped on every human person at conception.

This idolatrous tendency is part of our fallen human nature. To give into it only deepens the chasm between us and them. For such a tendency helps us to rigidly redraw the walls of division that Jesus paid dearly to destroy. Alternatively, a more faithful rendition of the Christian life is one lived out in a manner that reflects the true nature of Christ. For this provides us with the greatest opportunity to clearly reflect the expressed likeness of the Incarnate One in a world direly in need of such loving representation.

Biblical Motifs

Christian Scripture does not fail to note the reality of the Will to Power as an essential element of fallen Creation. Nor does is ignore efforts to recreate God in our image and bring God down to our level. Further, it provides evidence of the pervasive nature of the phenomenon. It did not begin with the Fall of humankind but is intrinsic to the very nature of evil that is lodged within the "prince of the power of the air,"[36] who uses his influence to try to undermine every human relationship and, thus, disrupt the project of bringing the Kingdom of God into present reality.

Satan's Rebellion

The biblical theme of entrenched Will to Power's continued encroachment is first vividly portrayed in the rebellion of Satan and the insurgence of this created one against the One by whom he had been created. Discontent with his already lofty position, Satan sought higher elevation. For though probably senior to most, if not all, other created beings, there was still One he perceived as higher. He could not, therefore, be satisfied. It was unacceptable to him that the image

---

[36]Eph 2:2

of any other being could outshine his own. Or that the image of the other—and not his—would be the pattern for humankind.

To be higher than other created beings was not enough for Satan. There remained One in his way and he was determined to surpass that One. And so, he set out to dislodge the Creator and bring God down to his level. Yet, this seriously misguided miscalculation proved to be costly.

How you have fallen from heaven,
O star of the morning, son of the dawn!
You have been cut down to the earth,
You who have weakened the nations!

But you said in your heart,
'I will ascend to heaven;
I will raise my throne above the stars of God,
And I will sit on the mount of assembly
In the recesses of the north.

I will ascend above the heights of the clouds;
I will make myself like the Most High'[37]

In Satan's striving to surpass the unsurpassable, he sacrificed the opportunity for the most intimate relationship possible. In patterning our assessment of God after Satan's failed attempt, we too, sacrifice the opportunity for complete intimacy and community with the other and with God. Satan's discontent and efforts to pass that dissatisfaction on to humankind are seen in the biblical narrative of the Fall. What Satan tempted Eve with was the possibility of moving out of her ordered place as a created being and becoming "like God,"... "knowing good and evil."[38] The temptation Satan presented was to

---

[37]Isa 14:12-15

[38]Gen 3:4

make God like the woman, to bring God down to her level, knowing no more good or no more evil than she did. The goal of this option was to domesticate God

Satan enticed Eve into believing in the possibility of being equal to God – a project in which he had already failed miserably. And that failure graphically illustrates the futility of our efforts to bring God down to our level no matter how hard we continue to try.

The Pharisees

Within the Lukan narrative, the prayer of the Pharisee "Thank God I am not like [these other people]."[39] This pious man saw those who did not follow his strict religious regimen as impure, and unworthy to stand in God's presence. He did not comprehend the filthiness of his own claimed righteousness but saw all those others as, inherently, unclean. It was to "some people" like him "who trusted in themselves that they were righteous, and viewed others with contempt"[40] that Jesus told this parable:

> *Two men went up into the temple to pray, one a Pharisee and the other a tax collector. The Pharisee stood and was praying this to himself: 'God, I thank You that I am not like other people: swindlers, unjust, adulterers, or even like this tax collector. I fast twice a week; I pay tithes of all that I get.*[41]

And none of what this man spoke was impressive to a God who does not look at the outward appearance of our actions and pronouncements to judge our righteousness, but rather looks on the attitude of our heart. As Jesus continued the parable, to further illustrate his point,

---

39Lk 18:11

40Lk 18:9

41Lk 18:10-14

But the tax collector, standing some distance away, was even unwilling to lift up his eyes to heaven, but was beating his breast, saying, 'God, be merciful to me, the sinner!'[42]

Jesus' declaration that [the tax collector] went to his house justified rather than [the Pharisee] for everyone who exalts himself will be humbled, but he who humbles himself will be exalted,"[43] underlies an important truth about our futile attempts to justify ourselves at the expense of others. The Pharisee commended himself to God as somehow, better and more deserving of God's grace than those he identified as less than himself. Though we, like this Pharisee, might consider these other people – swindlers, unjust, adulterers, or a tax collector – morally corrupt, his prayer does not take seriously our own sinfulness before God for a variety of infractions.

Within extra-biblical material, the ancient Hebrew prayer, "Blessed are [Y]ou for not making me a Gentile, a woman, or a slave,"[44]parallels Jesus' parable. It reinforces the sense of superiority that separates those who consider themselves as more deserving of God's favor than others. For each person identified in these prayers, is considered as, in some way, tainted and, therefore, less worthy of God's grace. They are sensed as less deserving of consideration as a full spiritual member of the dominant community. A privilege of our birth is to have not been born as one of them. This privilege, we tell ourselves, makes us more reflective of the image of God. It is the warrant for a level of dignity and respect that need not be accorded to the other.

---

[42]Lk 18:13

[43]Lk 18:14

[44]This ancient prayer that originated outside of the Jewish community appeared in the Talmud as early as the second century BCE and eventually became part of the tradition.

Nation against Nation

Jesus' assertion that, in the last days, "nation will rise against nation, and kingdom against kingdom,"[45] was not a prescription for aggressive promulgation of the gospel message or an invitation to advancement against the Roman government. Rather it was prophetically descriptive of a future in which every generation, from biblical times on, has continued to carry on a pattern of increasingly higher levels of the aggression already in evidence as he spoke these words. For Jesus was aware that, his sacrificial offer toward human reconciliation, would never bring about a period in human history when all of us could simply get along.

There has never been a moment in that history, prior to, during, nor after, the biblical era in which some faction of the human family has not been engulfed in conflict, or literally at war with another. Sometimes, the hostility has escalated to such an extent that several nations have been involved in combat at one time.[46] In many cases, moreover, both sides lay claim to identification as "Christian." And, in numerous cases, such aggression has been carried out in the name of Christ or of his church.

Within this religious context, those involved in these conflicts, see themselves as defending a faith, that, ostensibly, could not stand on its own. All sides regularly declare themselves as fighting on God's side, while destroying untold numbers of lives, emaciating entire communities, and causing mass human dislocation in the world that God so loved. Still, in the end, the cause of destruction has as much, if not more, to do with cultural, economic or national self-interest as with God's agenda of Kingdom building.

The Apostle James offers some insight into the state of human affairs that gives rise to the Will to Power within the intimate setting of Christian community. While there have been "just wars" waged on

---

45 Lk 21:10

46 For example, the Hundred Years War, and the First and Second World Wars.

behalf of oppressed communities, he insists that human avarice and lusting for what we do not have leads us to covet and murder to attain what we feel deprived of.[47] The devastation of war is the clearest indication that the motivation for the Will to Power has little to do with protecting a less fortunate group, or the good of humanity. Mostly, we are motivated to guard our narrowly defined self-interest and a way of life that we see as the most faithful reflection of the Kingdom of God.

The more physically, intellectually and emotionally abled, certainly, see themselves as more able to carry God's image than those others. For we assume that the Creator or all that is good and perfect cannot be subject to, or dwell fully within, what we label imperfection. Assuredly, those who evidence any degree of physical, intellectual or emotional shortage or disruption cannot be the best – or even an acceptable – representation of that image. Importantly, like those who questioned Jesus about the man who was born blind, we look for the root cause of that differently ableness in some structural flaw within the community of their origin.[48] So for the sake of the rest of Creation, we feel justified in operating in the Will to Power to constrain them.

---

[47] Jas 4:1-3 (NKJV)

[48] Jn 9: 1-2

Negation and the Will to Power

... for the one who does not love his brother whom he has seen, cannot love God whom he has not seen. 1 Jn 4:20b

It is natural to suppose that the opposite of love is hate. As Christians, we are taught from childhood that we should not hate anyone – not our enemies, not those who harm us, nor those who use us for their own benefit. We are encouraged not to retaliate when someone does us wrong. And we come to understand that we should not return an eye for an eye, and are admonished, that we should always display Christian civility, no matter how much we are provoked by the presence of evil intent within the other.

And with, at least mental, concession to these difficult ideals, we come to believe that, surely, this posture is enough. Certainly, nothing else can be expected of us. At times, even these measures of graciousness stretch the limits of our patience. For we are satisfied when we escape the, often present, temptation to render evil for evil. If the harm is perceived to be deep enough, we leave our enemies to the discipline of God, hoping that the vengeance that God claims for God's self with eventually and justifiably (in our thinking) be meted out on them. We hope that God will take things into God's own hands and will exact retribution on our behalf.

Jesus' commendation for us to love our neighbor goes far beyond refraining from doing evil to those who do evil to us and not harming those whom we consider our equals. Even that less difficult effort misses the mark of genuine love. Love is a dynamic, active verb. One cannot, truly, love passively. One can never genuinely love dispassionately. Love is the *intentional* seeking of the goodwill of the other. It involves the deliberate giving of oneself to the other in an act of generosity at one's own expense. The Apostle Paul spells out the dimensions of genuine love. It is more than a warm, fuzzy feeling. It is patient, it is kind, it is unselfish, it rejoices in the success of the other, it is forbearing and does not keep score of wrongdoing.[49]

God's standard is high and, on the surface, seemingly unattainable. And it most unattainable without the Spirit's assistance. The commendation to love those who hate you requires specific action. "Do good to those who misuse you, and "pray [earnestly] for those who use you out of spite."[50] This does not sound, at all, like indifference. Such an attitude requires the active pursuit of the welfare of an individual (or community) with whom we are at odds.

Jesus is clear that it does not require much effort to love those who love us[51]—those who are most like us, and, who return to us the same level of assistance that we grant them. This is expected of us. It is not difficult to do good to those who do good to us. It is only fair; it is anticipated. Further, reciprocity keeps the chain of their good actions toward us in place. This reciprocal formula has obvious benefits for both parties that make the effort worth it. Whether the return is material, spiritual or emotional, we both gain from the exchange in ways that have value for us. And this gain makes it possible, if not always easy to make the exchange.

---

49 I Cor 13:

50 Lk 6:26-28

51 Matt 5:46

Jesus is also insistent that we exhibit this same character of love in return to those who not only cannot assist or add to us, but who could, potentially, harm us—those who overpower and power over us. If it were, simply, a directive to love those from whom nothing good may come it would be difficult enough. But to go further and clearly insinuate that we extend this same love—not just the absence of hatred—to those who wish us harm or even engineer our demise—our enemy is an extraordinary requirement. These are those persons who exercise the Will to Power over us in some way.

Within the natural scale of understanding, to actively love those from whom we can expect harm—is absurd. It goes beyond everything the human inclination tells us. Indeed, in our own strength, it is impossible! And further, such an attitude or such actions would make us look foolish. It is a lofty-sounding goal, but who does that? Such an unnatural act is well beyond the powers that lie within us. It requires continued supernatural Holy Spirit. Empowerment. It requires a moment by moment renewing of the mind and dying to all that our natural inclinations dictate.

We are convinced we are doing what can be expected when we do them no, intentional, harm. When we, simply, let them go on with their lives and give them no regard. But that is not what Jesus required. Nor is it what Jesus demonstrated. Scripture reminds us that before we loved Him, He loved us. That while we were yet sinners and considered the enemies of God, in the ultimate act of love, Christ died for us.[52]

Resisting hatred does not fully fulfill the condition for love. It is the first step, the minimum requirement. Without moving away from hate, it is, impossible to love. But moving away from hate is not enough. While in resisting hating those who obviously deserve abhorrence, we feel we have done a great Christian thing, we are simply being civil.

---

[52]Rom 5:6

The parable of the good Samaritan proposes the answer to love's opposition.[53] The narrative vividly confronts us with what it means to love one's enemy. Those Jewish men who passed the wounded stranger lying in the street did not hate him. Indeed, he was one of them. Yet, he was among many nameless members of their community whom they did not know from any other unfortunate person in their city. Indeed, they intended him no harm, and did nothing, intentionally, to damage him. It was not their fault he had come on hard times. They simply left him, therefore, where they found him, not knowing or caring whether he lived or died.

As Jesus related, in the first instance, a priest happened to be going down the same road, overly busy with his priestly responsibilities so "when he saw the man, he passed by on the other side.[54] It would have been inconvenient to deter from his religious errands to stop to assist someone who might require too much of his time or take him off his intended course.

Shortly, a Levite, who also probably had heavy religious responsibilities, "came to the place and saw him [and also] passed by on the other side."[55] He, too, was probably overburdened with the critical tasks of his position. After all, there was the Temple to tend to and rituals for which to prepare. Taking care of wounded citizens was not in his position description, or on his orderly list of what had to be accomplished that day.

Neither leader passed over the wounded man in abhorrence over who or what he was or the state in which they found him. They were not turned off by his bloody condition. Instead, while each man was doing their regular religious responsibilities, they did not consider this other person a worthy focus of their attention. There was too much else to occupy it, so they disregarded the man and his situation. And in doing so, they negated his humanity.

53Lk 10:30-37

54Lk 10: 31

55 Lk 10: 32

Perhaps they thought that, sooner or later, someone of less importance, with less responsibility, or who was used to carrying out such lowly tasks for such lowly folk, would stop and render aid. As there were many within their sphere with some mundane need, it would be unreasonable to expect them to minister to them all. After all, there was probably a community hierarchy and, unfortunately, the poor fellow fell at the bottom of the pecking order, with seemingly, no intrinsic worth. He, therefore, was left to die.

As in this man's case, too often, the thing that kills is not the direct injury – but neglect by those who fail to attend to that injury. A small wound treated properly can heal quickly. That same wound, left unattended and exposed, may cause a person to bleed to death or die from the infection. Many cancers, if caught and attended to in the early stages may be completely curable. Unacknowledged and left untreated, these same cancers become a major threat to life.

The culprit is negation; the failure to recognize and address the very real personhood and need of the other. The collective objectification of members of a community as an inhuman lump renders the welfare of the entire group and its individual members of no consequence, relieving us of any need for concern or a sense of guilt regarding their circumstances. After all, we convince ourselves, they are who they are and where they are through no fault of ours. We have not, personally, done anything to harm them, so we are not responsible for their relief. We come to see the effort required to render any genuinely effective assistance as beyond what should reasonably be expected of us and taking us too far from our agenda.

The two men who passed by the stranger were so engrossed in their religious duties that they simply overlooked him. They did not acknowledge his humanity and treated him as if he did not exist. As if, his problem was just that—his problem—and of no concern to them. After all, they were not medical professionals, so what real assistance could they give.

Surprisingly, the man's aid came from a completely unexpected quarter. A despised Samaritan, someone to whom he, himself, would probably not have given the time of day, not only stopped and looked after him, but arranged for him to be cared for, and nursed back to health. The Samaritan showed mercy and godly compassion to someone who might not have done the same for him had circumstances been reversed – someone who might have considered him the enemy.

The religious ones' actions illustrate clearly that negation—the denial of another person's essential need or very existence—can be as deadly as hatred. Left unacknowledged, that need grows and festers like cancer, and becomes an avoidable flash point. Failing to take the other into account as a human being, fully created in the image of God and embodying the dignity and worth inherent in such creation, psychologically or spiritually nullifies them so they cease to exist for us. We, therefore, are relieved of considering them in any equation we construct to justify our existence, since we surmise that the outcome of our decisions is inconsequential for them. Or we estimate that those consequences do not really matter for, as non-entities, their existence is of no real significance to us.

At face value, benign neglect, the simple failure to acknowledge a person's full humanity and dignity, does not appear to be harmful. We simply let people alone even to the point of their destruction. Their blood is not on our hands, for we have not lifted a finger to harm them. Surely, they are not the neighbor whom we are called to love as ourselves. They are simply the faceless, insignificant other.

But Jesus illustrates the untenable foundation of this way of thinking. He was not, simply, chiding those who hated their neighbor. Instead, his words challenge those of us who fail to genuinely love our neighbor. The neighbor the two men passed on the road received care from one least likely to give it—a Samaritan whom they—and possibly the wounded stranger considered a half-breed. For within Jesus' time and culture, the Samaritan and Jew had little dealings with each other.

In ordinary situations, at the least, their lives would have been of no consequence for each other, and the Samaritan could have easily categorized the man lying on the road as his enemy.

As we read the parable of the good Samaritan, again, Jesus did not rebuke those who passed by the victim because they hated him, his concern was that they simply failed to consider him. They ignored him and his condition. He was not important to them.

In failing to love the neighbor, we know nothing of them, accept the myths and rumors we have heard, and we find them and their circumstances too inconsequential to make the effort to learn more. It is too costly to invest time, intellectual capital or social energy in gaining knowledge about them. For, getting to know them as individuals gives their existence too much weight. It causes us too much psychic discomfort, pushing us to give credence to their claim to be as fully human and created in the image of God as we are.

Still, in another place, Jesus injunction is even stronger and more difficult to come to terms with when he says to those of us who will hear,

> *...love your enemies, do good to those who hate you, bless those who curse you, pray for those who mistreat you.*[56]

These words leave us to wrestle with a seemingly impossible task, yet he reiterates several verses later, "Love your enemies, and do good..."[57] Everything within us rails against this and nothing within us resonates with this.

Jesus was deliberate in coupling love with supplication and the doing of good on behalf of those who are our adversaries. Just as faith without works is dead, alleged love without doing good, without actively seeking the welfare of the other is useless. Truthfully, this hard

---

[56]Lk 6:27-28.

[57]Lk 6:35.

requirement is a standard that we often fail to meet. But we cannot simply dismiss Jesus' command, as invalid idealism. We must grapple with the element of the Will to Power that is lodged within us to draw us away from the realization of that goal.

We cannot, then, congratulate ourselves for not hating. Jesus' ultimate sacrifice on behalf of a community that despised him, graphically displays the seriousness with which he made this claim on our obedience. For while we were yet sinners, and completely alienated from God, God sent his Son to die for us and that Son willingly surrendered his life on our behalf.

We cannot, moreover, allow ourselves to believe we have passed the test of Christian love, simply because we have fulfilled the letter of the Apostle Paul's treatise to the Corinthian church.[58] We are not so easily off the hook merely because we have abstained from being impatient, we have not been unkind, we have not been harsh, or jealous, or boastful.

The Apostle Paul offers further clarity on the substance of genuine love. Such love is not only patient, kind and gentle to those who are affable. It does not keep account of the wrongs done to us by others who, measured in frail human terms, are less lovely or downright unlovable. Authentic love does not seek opportunities to repay them for their ill-doing, and so to get a hand up on them. [59]

A major aspect of God-imaged createdness is the desire for deep, genuine relationship—to be in authentic human community. Human flourishing—and more the flourishing of human community—depends upon connection. To withhold relationship from the other is to contribute to the sense of negation.

Too often we excuse ourselves from the truth of our sinfulness in this area, simply asserting that we have not hurt anyone. In our

---

[58]I Cor 13

[59]I Cor 13:5

assessment, our hands are clean for we are not accountable for our mothers' and fathers' sins.[60] In truth, however, we are blood guilty of the sin of omission. That we have not intentionally caused harm is noteworthy. Yet, in more cases, neither have we helped to ameliorate their injustice or suffering. Further, we stood by and watched, acting either as if those experiencing injustice do not exist, or that the injustice that they suffer is inconsequential.

Without a trace of remorse, we allow them to perish or be vilified, pretending all the while that we do not see or hear them. And to soothe our conscience, we have worshipped a God who appears to us to be as inattentive to their plight as we are. For while we dismiss any preferential option for those who are suffering as idolatrous, we title our fortunate situation election and exceptionalism.

The episode of America slavery excellently portrays the quality of negation. While the harsh cruelty of slavery itself was enough, the elaborate system created to undermine the slaves' personhood was even more dehumanizing. To add to the insult, the political decision to count each slave as only three-fifths of a human being,[61] relegated them to the category of a sub-human super animal. This decision was not made to cause more physical harm to the person. An inherent consequence, though, was the removal of any moral necessity to treat the individual as fully human, and the removal of any legal accountability for those who failed to do so.

Jesus never admonished his listeners, "do not hate your enemy." If he had simply said that, many, if not most, Christians could easily

---

[60] And it might well be, as in the case of slavery, that it is our father's treatment of them that has made them our enemies.

[61] According to the Three-Fifths Compromise proposed by James Wilson and Roger Sherman, the concession reached among state delegates during the 1787 United States Constitutional Convention allowed slaves to be counted as three-fifths in total when apportioning Representatives, as well as Presidential electors and taxes. With the Thirteenth Amendment to the Constitution enacted in 1865 to outlaw slavery, the Three-Fifths Compromise was rendered obsolete.

pass that test. "I' do not hate anyone," we could comfortably insist. But truthfully, there are few people we genuinely love. And our failure to acknowledge a person's full humanity and dignity equates with hatred, for the effects of these two attitudes are, often, devastatingly similar.

Again, Jesus did not simply challenge us not to curse those who curse us. Going beyond that, he insisted that we, "love [our] enemies, bless those who curse [us], do good to those who hate [us], and pray for those who spitefully use… and persecute [us].[62] For Christians then, it is insufficient to abstain from hating, for such a posture does not equate to genuine love. Such love is not, merely, the absence of loathing or a negative response. Our response could be deadly neutral. We could fail to act when action is required to save a life or provide for a desperate need. Though not actively participating in the other's demise, we passively allow it to unfold.

The Jewish Holocaust blatantly exemplifies the negation of a people during a time of extreme need. Though the actual atrocities were carried out by Hitler's regime, Germany became a convenient scapegoat for anti-Semitic sentiments of the Christian community, as the church silently watched millions of Jews and other "undesirables" meet a horrendous end. Those who could have responded to the plight of these others acted as it were of no consequence. For what was happening to the Jewish people was a self-contained catastrophe that bore little on the daily lives of those initially outside Hitler's path of destruction. So, the world stood by, as it had done on many occasions, as the genocide of a people was systematically carried out. Yet while our failure to assist assured their destruction, we could say, we did nothing to hurt them.

Such stories have been repeated throughout history, on a national and global scale, as well as in individual encounters with those who are somehow unlike or do not benefit us. Thousands of blacks were

---

62 Matt 5:42-44

lynched and the rights of hundreds of thousands more were abrogated while the church stood silently. Native Americans. Latino immigrants, tribal and territorial wars in Africa, Asia, and the Middle East: the unending list of atrocities has often drawn the same response—it is not our problem. We mean them no harm, but we easily cross the intellectual and spiritual street to escape dirtying our hands with the messiness of their situation.

The slaves could be viewed as property since any genuine reflection of the image of God in these dark, mysterious creatures was denied, as was any possibility of their being full spiritual beings. After all, slave owners reasoned, their property could not be as close to God, or, as loved by God as they were for, surely, they did not merit the same consideration.

While a few non-slave holders saw the abolition of slavery as essential or viable, for decades, Northern white Christians regarded Southern slavery as a regional issue of no import to them. Only when that issue threatened the nation's unity, did they take sides. As with many issues the silence of both the Northern and Southern churches was deafening. And when a voice was proffered, it often fell on the wrong side. Biblical narratives were concocted to support slavery and foisted on the slaves as their introduction to Christian faith. These accounts were crafted to quell any objections from other Christians who might exhibit a modicum of conscience about slavery. They also were intended to invoke a level of docility and patient endurance among those slaves who might be tempted to actively seek redress.

Contemporary white Americans' insistence of no culpability for a moral system that bankrupted black socio-cultural and economic stability for centuries when they have done nothing to constrain it, exemplifies such a stance. Failure of many men to acknowledge the global reality of blatant sexism and misogyny is another example. Bemoaning the unfortunate outcome of situations when we could help ameliorate them renders us like the religious men who passed by the fallen stranger and left him to the good Samaritan. For we often find ourselves too religiously busy to reach out to the stranger whose welfare is unimportant to us. Without raising a finger to harm them, we fail to offer the assistance that would help them move beyond the harmful situation. The other becomes the scapegoat for everything that is wrong in the world. And so, we leave them alone to their own destruction.

The downward spiral from negation to hatred is easy. The first step is shifting from indifference to blame by excusing ourselves from any complicity in their situation. "If those people would get themselves together," we tell ourselves, "everything would be different." We would not be continuously reminded of their plight and could get on with our lives. After all, we convince ourselves, it is there fault that they are where and how they are. We did not put them there, so surely, we cannot be expected to discomfort ourselves to help them.

We move from blame to irritation. It bothers us that their plight gets so much attention when our perceived needs appear to go, largely, unnoticed. We are concerned that those who once wholeheartedly supported our project have begun to question our common understandings and goals. We see them targeting the limited resources for which we have fought toward ameliorating the plight of the other. We sense that what we claim as our due and label as undeserved entitlements for the other is being squandered.

We slide from irritation to distrust of their agenda. Our alleged affirmation that all men [and women] are endowed by the Creator with the 'inalienable right" to "life, liberty and the pursuit of happiness," does not relieve us of irritation by their continued agitation for these rights. We wish that they would just be quiet about any perceived abrogation of those rights. Any complaint about their condition is considered unfounded aggression and a personal threat. For we see them as using their situation to take away what is justly ours.

Distrust slips into hostility that seethes just below the surface. When their plight is, continually, brought up, we angrily dismiss it as wholly fabricated and having no basis. Through the eyes of this hostility, every gesture is suspect and nothing they do pleases us.

This anger finally evolves into hatred. Not always blatant hatred, for, as Christians or other religious persons, we are afraid of seeming unloving or uncompassionate and never want to be labeled as such. Instead, we covertly develop attitudes—isms—that express themselves in subtle, clandestine actions. We create, seemingly, pious platitudes that do not aid them or rob us of our comfort in negating them. This charade of Christian piety is, perhaps, the most despicable element of the Will to Power for the individual believer.

This evolution is usually slow and subtle—sometimes, imperceptible to those who are inattentive. Finally, such hatred may pass as passion for a cause. We are not fighting against them, and we mean them no harm—as if there were no real human costs involved in our disinterest.

For we do not attempt to engage members of those communities as genuine God-imaged human beings. *They*—as we refer to the individual members of the other group—share a common flaw, no matter how diverse the path that led to it.

It goes against everything in the human psyche to "regard one another as more important than oneself.[63] But stopping short of that, the effort required to consider the other as on par with us is only slightly less difficult. Building on our tendency to re-create God as a caricature of ourselves, we assume that any root cause of deficiency or distress in the other must lie, entirely, within them.

Instead of understanding ourselves as participating in furthering God's project of Kingdom building – modeling the Kingdom of God on earth, we conveniently see God as a helper of our project. God's primary purpose, then, becomes assisting us to fulfill our deepest longing purpose. Furthermore, any attention we—or God—pays to them is an unnecessary distraction from our project.

---

[63] Phil 2:3

THE LIES WE TELL OURSELVES

"The heart is deceitful above all things, And desperately wicked;
Who can know it? Jer 17:9

Continuing to carry out our project of self-preservation and reimaging God as ourselves requires enormous effort. The thing we disdain most in the other is lodged just under our skin, waiting to express itself the moment we let down our defenses. For, if told the truth, if we could exchange places with our detractors, we would subject them to the same treatment they have imposed on us. We would be dismissive of them and inattentive to their situation. We would power over them. Indeed, vestiges of the attribute we most disparage in the other are evident in almost every action or attitude we express toward them. For when we see what we loathe in those who are perceived, in some way, to hold power over us, we also see a reflection of what we could become if we were left to our own devices and could trade places with them. When we see what we loathe in those over whom we hold power, we see what we could become if the props were pulled from under us.

A most unfortunate thing about the persistence of the Will to Power is our need to concoct lies to keep us from acknowledging its existence. Our fallenness impairs our ability to discern its depth and how far we are from any supposed measure of perfection. For our involvement in the Will to Power is so abhorrent we dare not face it head-on, lest we see ourselves for what we are and become devastated by that realization.

The lies, delusions, and myths we fabricate or continue to sustain are too numerous to delineate completely. Every instance of Will to Power requires nuancing an untruth to make it palatable. Moreover, the fabrication must appear to be rational and believable. The lie starts simply, becoming more complex as the danger of encroachment appears more threatening. The assertion of innocence becomes insistence that the problem is lodged in them and grows into an unshakeable conviction of ontological difference between us and them that renders them deserving of everything they are getting.

We are innocent

Some measure of privilege derives from any one of several factors. Race, gender, class position or religious affiliation all can be criteria for the allocation and consumption of advantage within a society. Assuredly, some are launched into socio-economic, or political, prominence by an "accident" of birth, and continue to have access to that privilege, whether ever taking advantage of it. Such privilege accrues to them by the very nature of their being, and is, in some way, always available to them. Yet, many in this position excuse themselves from collective culpability in the ongoing receipt of that privilege. Indeed, many with inherent privilege are oblivious to the breadth of the unearned advantage, as well as, to the way such privilege is built into the fabric of every oppressive system.

Such an existence is as natural as breathing to those born to it and is part of the systemic isms that make up our culture. Each layer of privilege exists in relationship to every underlying layer. The lie about our innocence in complicity with privilege exhibits itself in many ways.

Within Western culture, black men refer to whites as racist, yet exercise considerable advantage over almost every other racial or cultural group. Further, they, like all men, enjoy a measure of privilege from simply being male. And many white women who decry sexism, often condescend to black, Latino and Asian women, treat them with disdain, and disregard their contribution to the pursuit of equality.

At one level, individuals in inherited positions of power are not the real problem. Systemic, entrenched othering is the culprit. Still, they benefit from those systems to varying degrees. And few completely denounce, disavow or fail to take advantage of the privilege of accrued power, in some way. As an African American woman, historically, there are privileges that have accrued to me, simply based on my citizenship. So as loudly as I decry the racial bigotry that characterizes the essence of my American, experience, within the global context, I have benefited from the same privilege that has been available to other Americans.

Those born into privilege do not, necessarily, request to be treated with deference. Such treatment automatically accrues to them because of their perceived place in the social order. Whether they ever exercise the privilege, it accrues to them by the circumstances of birth. Yet, they always have the choice of acknowledging that privilege or pretending it does not exist. They can use it to their benefit and the detriment of others or they can employ it for others' benefit.

When viewed globally I am among those who have a degree of wealth. For the poverty that even the poorest American experiences is relative deprivation. Through the lens of meager subsistence many in the two-thirds world experience, while my black womanhood often renders me second, this demeaning reality is incomparable to that of women around the globe who are regularly subjected to dehumanizing, life-threatening practices.

The Problem is Them

Black people, consistently, tell themselves the lie that only white people are racist. For, they narrowly define racism as prejudice with power. The simple definition of racism, however, is holding some races as ontologically—at the core of their existence—better than others and governing our attitudes and actions according to that belief. Racism involves not just overt or oppressive attitudes and actions, but those that are covert as well. Yet were the first definition accurate, the fundamental belief is that the only genuine powers are economic and political. We all, however, have a measure of power, as well as the capacity to exercise that power over the other. As women, we tell ourselves that we cannot be sexists. Or those who are poor claim they do not discriminate against others because of economic status.

Such assertions are based on a false premise that we are innocent of what it takes to Will to Power. But how quickly, when given the opportunity, victims of oppression become oppressors.

So often our first response to another human being is as belonging to a group, with no distinction about individual flaws or imperfections. When we encounter the other at a significant level, our conviction that the entire group is deficient in ways lets us keep them at arms' length. This makes it easier to judge quickly, if not accurately, based on what we see and hear. These shallow disengaged judgments, principally, serve to reinforce our many prejudices. The least important features of our humanity: skin color, gender, accent, manner of dress, body structure, even personal habits, become, seemingly, obvious confirmation that we have judged the other correctly. We do not need, then, to objectively engage the individual. Or, our interactions are tainted by underlying assumptions of social, psychological, intellectual or spiritual deficiency. Frivolous, unimportant characteristics that in no way indicate a person's intrinsic worth serve as the basis for first level judgments of their ontological value that carry through in our ongoing encounters.

All of this is understandable in some way. We are, always, inundated with social, cultural and psychic cues that make such first level judgments unavoidable. We have been told through family conversations, misguided educational efforts, theological misrepresentations, and media exposure, that something is wrong with them. Such cues are reinforced by a singular or multiple negative interaction with single members of the other group that leave a lasting impression.

Such cues, as off-target as they are, have often proven helpful in protecting us from compromising situations. Or at least we can justify such an argument as we negotiate the intricate social relationships that make up our reality. These cues release us from dealing with intricate human subtlety to allow us to efficiently manage brief exchanges in a manner least harmful to us and get on with our lives. Knowing and discerning at a deeper level of shared human experience requires more intentionality than we are inclined to invest. In the moment, it does not matter that we miss opportunities for a more meaningful encounter. We do not have time for that. For, should we gain information about them, the possibility for individualization grows and the excuses for disinterest evaporate.

Yet, too often, these negative responses go uncorrected for extended periods of time. Even after repeated encounters with an individual or group highlights intersections where we have more in common than we have differences, we continue to limit the level of engagement we offer to them. We continue to set uncrossable boundaries around them over which we do not invite them – because of their unshakeable group identity. New information about them, is not enough to dismantle our presuppositions, so we never completely trust them.

Moreover, the mental tapes we continually replay, remind us that if they attempt to become like us it could not, possibly, be because they admire us. Rather, they want to take advantage of us. They are not trying to identify strengths to emulate, but rather to identify weaknesses to exploit. They want to continue to put up barriers to block our liberation. We insist that to show them any vulnerability exposes us to further oppression. For we are convinced that, though pretending it to be so, they have no real appreciation for us.

We are Ontologically Different

We must continue to deceive ourselves to sustain the illusion that any perceived ontological different is inbred. If we remain convinced that they are in some way inferior – or superior, we can maintain our stance about them with no guilt or remorse. After all, if we can point to the privilege they hold, our attitude toward them is justified. If we can point to the lack they exhibit, it is, at least in part, their fault, as a member of their group, since they are, in some manner, deficient. This posture relieves us from having to take their situation seriously.

It is not possible to hold ourselves harmless and support systemic oppression unless we convince ourselves that the DNA of the other is not simply different, it is, in some significant way, deficient. To see them otherwise and realize that, like us, they are simply part of fallen, flawed humanity forces us to admit our complicity in this oppression.

From a biblical perspective, however, the genetic disposition and DNA for all races (ethnic groups) and both genders could be found in Adam – the first human being. Further, that disposition and DNA could be found in Noah and the members of his family, since all the rest of the human family had previously been destroyed. Indeed, the passages following the Flood narrative delineate the beginning of the major ethnic groups directly out of Noah's three sons, portraying no hierarchical system, but a familial structure of equals.

Yet, as the mental tapes are replayed, we hear what we have always heard and come to believe, through community wisdom: none of them is ever completely trustworthy. None of them can ever be allowed to get to close too us. They can be colleagues, associates, or fellow congregants, but, at the end of the day, never intimate friends. For they, still, are not entirely like one of us and they never can be.

On the one hand, they have not been where we have been and can never go there. They have not participated in our suffering and sense of alienation. They cannot, therefore, possibly understand our pain, shame, or insecurities. On the other hand, they have not been able to avail themselves of the privileges of our birth, the refinements of culture that have lifted us to a morally, mentally or psychically higher plane. And they never will. Yet, we know that even if they were able to share our experience or avail themselves of such privilege, they could never fully overcome the inbred deficiency of birth or disadvantage of their culture. They would still be lacking in some easily discernable, and essential quality.

Slave masters convinced themselves that the people they confiscated from Africa lacked a fully developed human soul. Holding this myth allowed them to subjugate their captives, physically and mentally abuse and use them, as property, for profit with a clear conscience. The absence of, otherwise, attendant guilt allowed them to treat another person created fully in God's image in a dastardly manner—as if he or she were an animal. Holding to this myth, they could reap substantial benefit from the dehumanizing treatment they inflicted on other human beings while proclaiming an earnest affirmation of Christian faith.

Secondly, when a black person assumes that *all*—not just some, or even most—white people, as a group, are inherently racist as part of the fabric of their being—as if racism is genetically encoded, they invoke the very the prejudice they decry. The lie is that white people (as a group) cannot be trusted – and, at the extreme end—must be feared. The unfortunate myth perceives white people (as a community) as inherently prejudiced and incapable of treating black people fairly. The list of generalizations is long: "White people (as a whole) are obviously less spiritual." "White people (as a whole) are only interested in money." "White people (as a whole) are never sincere in their dealings with people of color."

Those men who have, historically, oppressed women had to convince themselves that women were inherently inferior. Only such a delusion allows them to deny women a modicum of respect and, implicitly, denigrate them as sexual objects. Adhering to this allows men to dismiss women as only good for serving at their pleasure without considering these women's authentic needs and to negate women's desire for authentic intimacy as weakness.

Traditionally "nice" women are regarded either as pristine, untouchable objects with no appetite for base sexual pleasure. Or, they are treated as little more capable than children, needing supervision and guidance from some male—a parent, sibling, spouse or significant other, or intervention by a societal entity. Still, such women are viewed as manipulative seducers who use men for material support and who, in return, deserve to be used for the sexual gratification they provide.

Strong women who dare to demand equal treatment, on the other hand, are often branded as unfeminine, masculine, or aggressive men haters. "Good women" are warned to stay away from them lest they are tainted by these bad attitudes. Or they are stigmatized with labels that render them persona non grata, keeping women who might benefit from their nurture away from them.

The biblical narrative of queen Vashti's refusal to capitulate to the unjust demands of her drunken husband, King Ahasuerus, that she display herself before a drunken hoard of revelers is an excellent example. Her audacity to own her personhood and defy the king, caused concern among his counselors, as the advice from his trusted aide, Memucan suggests:

> *Queen Vashti has wronged not only the king but also all the princes and all the peoples who are in all the provinces of King Ahasuerus. …the queen's conduct will become known to all the women causing them to look with*

contempt on their husbands by saying, 'King Ahasuerus commanded Queen Vashti to be brought in to his presence, but she did not come.'[64]

Such rhetoric has been used throughout the centuries to keep women "in their place. Modern iterations of extremes of the lie, target women who no longer tolerate subjugation, explicitly denigrate them as sexual objects, or vilify them with names that identify them with female dogs in heat.

Some men, on the other hand, may see all women as manipulative seducers who are only out to use men for the security and material possessions they offer. For them, women offer no real value, and the piece of themselves they are required to give up is simply the cost of doing business. The refutation of the lie no way diminishes the genuine harm done to women by oppressive, patriarchal systems to which they are regularly subjected. The media is rife with depictions of women as seductive, mindless entities whose primary value is to entice men to fulfill their own needs. But that does not make such a depiction an accurate reflection of the inherent nature or worth of a woman.

Within gendered relationships, however, sexism—the holding of stereotypic attitudes about the quality or worth of a person based, primarily, on gender goes both ways. Some women falsely hold to the myth that all men are patriarchal and misogynist. They conclude that men, as a group, are only interested in women as objects of their own male egos and pleasure. It is taught to us by our mothers and reiterated within ongoing conversations with friends, colleagues or complete strangers about the state of things as they are—or, at least, how we perceive them to be.

Failure to acknowledge the reciprocal nature of sexism removes us from the possibility of living out the intimate relational mutuality intended in our God-imaged creation. Male and female, together, reflect God's image, and such failure creates a perpetual climate in

---

[64]Esth 1:16-17

which the infamous "war of the sexes" often referred to offhandedly as the foundation for a situation comedy, is real, harsh and unending.

Women did not construct the stratified relational power hierarchy that supports the sexism, It was designed to keep them "in their place." It often takes its most drastic form in settings and cultures where men and women are already marginalized. In this way, men, who are already depreciated, gain the upper hand over at least one group, without feeling totally locked out of the power structure.

It is equally as simplistic to believe that class issues could be settled if those on the lower economic rung simply lived within their means and "pull themselves up" by their proverbial "bootstraps." This thinking removes any acknowledgment that the means of creation and distribution of wealth are often completely out of their hands. Or that entire an economic system has been set up to keep them in their place to benefit larger society. The entire class of people are poor, we tell ourselves, because they have not mastered the skill of managing their material resources. The reality that ninety percent of global wealth is in the hands of a minute percentage of the global population who live within narrowly delineated spheres escapes us. Without convincing ourselves that it simply has everything to do with our intellectual stamina and sheer resourcefulness, we cannot continue to absolve ourselves of our involvement in economic exploitation. Such a simplistic reading of engrained attitudes rejects serious consideration of generations of economic deprivation that lodges resources, or means of production and distribution, in the hands of a small minority of stakeholders who wield power over access of others to the necessary staples of life.

Elaborate myths are created on both sides. Some, such as "the curse of Ham," [65] justify the economic subjugation of an entire group

---

[65] The concept of the curse of Ham comes from a misunderstanding of the biblical narrative that relates Noah pronouncing a curse on Canaan, Ham's son and Noah's grandson after waking up the grandfather woke from a drunken, naked stupor and sensed that he had

while supporting the position at the top of the economic rung for the other. So, these concoctions serve double duty. They relieve the materially disadvantaged of any responsibility for their situation, since it is just the way things are. At the same time, they release the advantaged from any liability in the situation since, again, it is just the nature of things.

It is equally simplistic, however, to assume that all people of means are oppressors whose wealth could only come from exploiting others., that all of those who are advantaged have no regard for those who are less so. For such an assumption reiterates the Will to Power in assuming that the disadvantaged are somehow innately more spiritual and, therefore more deserving of God's favor.

Further, members of either group who do not buy into the lie are treated as traitors. For collective protection of either group from the perceived threat of encroachment is more important than truth. No member of the group is encouraged to think that it could be otherwise. To link or empathize with the other in any substantial manner is considered an act of treason.

The most unfortunate thing about such myths is that when told often enough, and with enough passion, both sides internalize them as reality. Victims adopt the negative untruth as self-blame, self-hatred, and hopelessness. Perpetrators, on the other hand, ascribe a level of sacred truth to them that, a priori, boast their assessment of themselves and serves as the support for all interactions with the other. Each side comfortably bases deep-seated attitudes, fears, and behaviors on nothing more than myths without violating deeply held moral and ethical ideals.

---

been dishonored by his son. The story may have originally been used to justify the Israelites subjugation of the Canaanites. Later, it was interpreted by some an explanation for slavery and the mistreatment of people of color, as well as internalized by some in the black community as a rationale from their inability to thrive economically, politically, or socially.

Abused women's excusing the abuser's behavior and questioning their own role in eliciting the abuse exemplifies the impact of these lies. Repeatedly, women insist that if only they had been a better lover, their partner or spouse would not have cheated on them. If only they had been a more submissive wife, they would not have suffered abuse. If they had been less seductive, they would not have been harassed or molested. If only they had the desirable qualities of their male colleagues, they would have been treated more fairly at work.

Without ever verbalizing these myths, they so easily become the negative self-talk we have with ourselves when nobody else is listening. This inner conversation convinces us that we are, at least in part, implicated in the problem. And this self-talk keeps us entrapped in dehumanizing circumstances that kill us emotionally, mentally, spiritually, and often, physically.

MANIFESTATIONS OF THE WILL TO POWER

No temptation has overtaken you, but such as is common to man

1 Cor 10:13

One of the most disconcerting features of the Will to Power is its ubiquity. It is everywhere—within every culture or society and in each of us—in some form. Though an individual is innocent of one ism, he or she is rarely untainted by some form of the universal human malady. Vestiges of the syndrome are independent of time, place, or situation. Their persistent presence testifies to the entrenched nature of the disorder and the difficulty in successfully dislodging remnants of the disorder from the human situation.

The way some level of the Will to Power is individually and collectively evident often surprises us. For, the othering that is its hallmark plays out variably in differing contexts. Its threads may subtly weave themselves into the woof and warp of the seemingly smooth fabric of everyday relationships. Or, it may blatantly operate in ways that produce psychological, mental, emotional, social, physical, economic, and/or spiritual harm to an entire community or nation. Often remnants of the trait may lay dormant or unnoticed in the fallow soil of our spirit and psyche for protracted periods. They can fester beneath the surface, waiting for the right conditions and the opportune moment to strike with surprisingly startling force.

Some aspects are universal; at least small vestiges of these traits are found in almost every culture. We find evidence of racial distinctions and some form of gender discrimination, or economic disparity, for example, in most contexts. Further, no pristine culture exists in which class distinctions and prejudice play no part.

Other aspects are culturally defined, or at least play out differently or more evidently in specific cultures. Sexism may be tolerated within personal relationships, but completely rejected in professional settings. Misogynous behavior, on the other hand, is considered totally intolerable in progressive cultural settings, while fully supported within others that are characterized as more traditional.

These forms are more tolerated within certain cultures since they offer intrinsic value for the perpetrators whose acceptance, justification, and support allow them to thrive. The lynching of black men in the American South could continue for decades, for example, because the ethical and legal system upheld it.

Some properties are more pronounced than others. In some ways, these are considered more acceptable or less damaging than more blatant elements. For example, what are considered racist jokes are acceptable among colleagues we trust understand them as mindless humor, but not deemed appropriate for our public audiences. What are considered racial slurs, on the other hand, are, somehow, less acceptable even in the former situation.

Yet, ultimately, in some form, a level of the Will to Power manifests itself, at various times, in each of us. Certainly, however, those who are more intentional about monitoring its presence are somewhat more successful in limiting its detrimental imprint on our relations. Still, when we let down our guard, the subtlety of its reassertion into our thoughts and actions surprises us. There are times, then, when we are unaware of the extent to which we have capitulated to its overreaching influence, for it finds ever new contexts through which to present itself and contaminate relations we work so hard to establish.

Levels of Will to Power

Stereotyping

The most elementary form of Will to Power is the simple act of ascribing certain (positive or negative) attributes to persons or groups as predictable ways of behavior in specified situations based solely – or primarily – on their group identity. Such simplistic assumptions disregard discrete individual qualities of group members because it is easier to base access for all people within the group on generalizations. This relieves us of the messy work of looking for appropriate cues when dealing with anyone who represents the group.

The idea, for example, that all non-Christians are morally deficient, and all Christians exhibit a higher ethical standard is a stereotype that history, repeatedly, has proven inaccurate. While we generally expect Christians to take the moral high ground, repeated scandals within the faith community demonstrate that this is not always the case. Christians, rather, possess an admixture of good and bad character traits. Martin Luther's assessment of Christian character as, simultaneously, encompassing both saint and sinner is sobering. Further, the path to Christian perfection is always paved with moral slippage, as well as progress, even among the most pious. At the same time, many Christians may be surprised that some of the world's most respected and beneficent leaders were never Christian or abandoned the Christian faith for another tradition. Malcolm X, Mahatma Gandhi, Abraham Lincoln, W. E. B. DuBois nor Julian Bond professed Christian faith, yet each accomplished considerable good on behalf of their communities as well as the global society.

Stereotypes can be trivial or crucial, having little or significant consequences for the people that hold them. Educated people can be viewed as snobs or overly esteemed in fields in which they have little knowledge. Or, we cast those with less formal education as ignorant or unlearned, when they may have a high level of natural intelligence or be well-read in several areas. Urban people can be seen as overly sophisticated or even stuck up. On the other hand, people from rural areas can be deemed as primitive or uncouth

Stereotyping brands individual members of a group as if they will consistently act in a certain manner in all cases. For us, they have no other choice, since that is who they are by virtue of group identity. We assume that they are either good or bad, intelligent or intellectually limited, reasonable or unreasonable, valuable or useless based on that identity.

Stereotyping represents intellectual laziness that fails to adjust attitudes and behaviors toward the person as an individual. It is unnecessary to expend the mental energy to know them since, to us, the stereotype explains everything significant about them. We can mentally dismiss them as unworthy of our attention, without acquainting ourselves with them as our equal, either demoting them to lower status undeserving of our attention or elevating them to an unreachable status without bothering to recognize their individual value.

Prejudice

Though inaccurate, stereotyping can be good or bad – positive or negative. We can overestimate moral virtues, physical power, or the intellectual acumen of an entire group and generalize them to each member within that group. Conversely, we can downplay these same values for the group and each of its members. Either extreme leads to miscues in our interactions, that rob us of opportunities to acquire a genuine appreciation for the individual. Yet stereotyping is simply holding ideas about who people are.

Prejudicial attitudes, on the other hand, suggest that since people are part of a specific group our actions toward them and interactions with them, should be guided by such knowledge. Prejudice involves, primarily negative, stereotypical attitudes that assume the less admirable traits of the group assessment are true for everyone—or at least most—who fall within it.

Prejudice may be inclusive or exclusive. Inclusive prejudice targets all individuals within the group with the negative stereotype. When black people sometimes consider all white people racist, and, approach each of them with disdain and distrust they exhibit inclusive prejudice. With exclusive prejudice, anyone who is not specifically apart of our reference group is summarily prevented from consideration. For example, men may carry the prejudicial attitude that women should be excluded from carrying out specific tasks, simply because they are not men and do not have the physical stamina or mental sharpness of men. Or they may hold that women should be paid less for the same work since they do not carry the same weight of being the family "breadwinner" as a man.

Most of us hold a degree of prejudice. We assume that members of our group—and not any other—are naturally, more authentically human—more humane, more intelligent, more spiritual, more motivated or more generous than members of other groups. They are whom we have counted them to be, and no amount of objective converse evidence changes our assessment. We suffice on circumstantial evidence that fuels our prejudice, and we are completely content that we are right.

As unfair as prejudice may be, however, even it can be a hidden, internal attitude that mostly constrains us to avoid the other. While these mindsets rob us of rich opportunities for interaction with people who are different–breaking the relational intimacy intended in Creation, they do not necessarily do material harm to the other individual or community.

Discrimination

Conversely, discrimination is the active working out of prejudicial attitudes–granting or withholding reward to others based entirely or primarily on prejudice toward them. It results in actively denying or limiting material opportunities in ways that affect the wellbeing of one group or unfairly benefit another.

While a person can mask prejudice, at times overcompensating for it, discrimination is the visible disclosure of deeply held prejudicial attitudes. Discrimination can occur intentionally when these attitudes lead us to believe that members of the other group deserve to be treated differently. Yet, discrimination may also occur involuntarily, when residual prejudicial attitudes naturally work themselves out.

In the first case, no excuse is made for intentional discriminatory behavior, for, after all, those on the receiving end should know their place, expect to be treated in a certain manner and agree with the perpetrator that they deserve it. Throughout the Jim Crow era, numerous discriminatory practices were put in place to remind black people of their second-class status and keep them from rising above it. Inferior educational resources, exclusion from employment opportunities, inferior infrastructure in black communities and biased judicial systems, all stood to remind black people of "their place"

Such direct discrimination specifically targeted toward a group has its corollary in indirect discrimination resulting from actions that appear to have the same impact on all parties, but disproportionately disadvantage or benefit members of one group. Within this context, practices that appear to be neutral, impartial or even equal, fail to bring equity to the disparate parties who are impacted by them. To insist that equal educational opportunities are available to all, for example, when the road to such education is structured in a manner that prevents certain groups from having access is indirect. Hidden, indirect, prejudice is, not so much, targeted at preventing the other group from attaining status or resources. Rather, it aims to protect those who fear the other, or future generations of their group, from losing their way of life.

Patronization

Other practices that seemingly appear to be in the interest of the target group, can, in actuality, be no more than patronizing or paternalistic. Patronization acts in an implicitly or openly condescending manner toward the other that fails to accord them full human capacity. Patronizing behavior ascribes intellectual, moral, or spiritual limitation that objectifies the other as needing our "care." At the same time, it exacts psychic acquiescence and/or a sense of material obligation from the other, expecting them to exhibit dependency and an attitude of gratefulness for the little that is allotted to them.

Patronization can masquerade as simply offering helpful solutions to a situation in which the other finds him or herself. But this offer of assistance requires relinquishing free moral agency to the other. The aim is either placating the other's felt need for resistance to oppression or reducing them to a child-like dependency that robs them of the opportunity to decide on their best course of action.

Paternalistic attitudes assume that without our help the subject group could not possibly make it. These attitudes allow us to provide the kind of assistance we have determined they need without giving credence to what group members sense is required. For we assume that they are too mired in the situation, or otherwise too deficient to know what is good for themselves. Programs and projects are created for them, based on our sense of what they need or what we would desire were we in their place. Importantly, these projects always fall short of providing the requisites for the other securing total liberation and becoming equal with us. Paternalism, therefore, directs seemingly well-intentioned benevolence toward a person or group in a manner that is, actually, intrusive.

Bigotry

Bigotry can be characterized as a general intolerance directed at all people who are part of any one of many groups in which one does not hold membership. Bigotry is expressed as supremacism – a generalized attitude that one's own group, is superior to all other groups and/or deserves to be treated with deference by members of all other groups. Such mindsets can be expressed as blatant hostility, total avoidance or psychic harassment.

Most people hold stereotypes of other groups in one form or another, and there may be many who have prejudicial attitudes or discriminate in some way. Further, many well-meaning people—even Christians—who fail to determine and fully consider the desires or ability of the other can become patronizing. The number of people who are truly bigoted, however, is small, especially within the Christian community. Yet, acts of bigotry could be as minor as labeling, name calling, or ignoring members of the other group when they should have our attention. Or, they might include such substantial transgressions as joining organizations whose aim is to intimidate or demoralize the other.

Bigoted people circle the wagons around themselves, closing themselves off from the possibility of any meaningful or protracted engagement that might render material benefit to the other. In the end, the ultimate aim of bigotry is to relieve oneself of interaction with members of the other group—allowing them to just go away to inhabit their own space. For the bigot desires to never have to transact meaningful commerce with the other as an equal player in the game of life.

Bigotry becomes vilification when we openly slander or publicly act in ways that encourage others to exhibit hatred or contempt or enact harm on others because of those attributes. An act as seemingly innocuous as making a comment on social or public media or giving a condemning speech can seemingly give license to carry out acts of intolerance or even violence.

Oppression

Individuals, groups or societies are oppressive when their bigotry drives them to carry out systematic sustained abuse, exploitation, and injustice directed toward the other in a manner that seeks to cause psychological, emotional, physical or economic harm, or to affect the other in ways that extract advantage for the perpetrator at their expense. Explicit oppression is blatantly extracted by the hands of the perpetrator to openly demoralize the other. Its aim is to render the other helpless in mounting a defense. Though prejudice against Jewish people has been present for centuries, it expressed itself most obviously as oppression during the pogroms carried out during the Nazi regime when a systematic program of deadly cruelty was lodged against an entire population. But oppression also may be a tool to wrest control of a valuable (tangible or intangible) asset the other is thought to hold such as the human labor capitol that slaves provided for plantation owners. In either case, oppression involves the deliberate effort to undermine the welfare of the other to render them harmless to or useful for us.

Oppression is rarely carried out by a solitary individual. It is, generally, a group action either carried out by a powerful oligarchy or by an entire segment of society. Laws are enacted, military resources are amassed, tariffs and sanctions are established. Conditions are made so intolerable that they temper the will and spirit of the other to fight against tyranny or they provoke a radical attempt to eradicate its cause.

The systematic nature of oppression shows that it does not come about as an unfortunate, unintended consequence of otherwise neutral practices. Rather oppression is calculatingly directed at those who, for one reason or another, cannot protect themselves. Complicit oppression, then, is more than, simple, benign neglect of the other; it involves the, considered, intentional decision not to intervene in the harm that is being carried out. The complicit oppressor, then, gives tacit, moral support for its insinuated or explicit rationale. So, silence, itself, can be oppressive.

Oppression exacts psychic or material loss from an individual or a group in ways that restrict full human flourishing. Someone must lose for someone else to gain. Someone or some group must surrender some portion of their full humanity for the other to sense that they are flourishing.

Genocide

The most extreme outworking and the harshest manifestation of the Will to Power is the strategic attempt to completely, or substantially, eliminate any threat from the other by deliberately imposing conditions that lead to their physical, mental or material destruction. While that destruction might be the immediate result of a targeted action or set of actions, it can be through gradual, sustained or even indirect action or a set of actions whose aim is to ultimately destroy the other.

Genocide can be accomplished through any number of strategies designed to bring about such destruction. As with the difference between the immediate death of a heart attack or the slow, painful, increasingly debilitating death of cancer, genocidal measures may not outrightly kill the other, but may cause a level of harm that renders the community incapable of full human flourishing and, finally, leads to psychic or spiritual the death of a significant number of its members.

Since the end goal of genocide is destroying the legacy of the community, genocide can be accomplished successfully by imposing one measure of several that destroys that community through attrition – causing it to eventually die out. Measures may be imposed to prevent birth or to disrupt the birth cycle by forced birth controlled or by isolating men and women from each other through involuntary conscription or mass incarceration. Other measures include introducing disease or other unbearable living conditions or promoting policies that encourage dysfunctional behavior within a group and which eventually bring about its decline.

Outright murder or massacre of communities is generally the method of last resort, since it is likely to draw the harshest response from those outside either community. Nevertheless, even these methods have been successfully employed against groups that are not valued by the broader society.

From the Christian vantage point, genocide is an unthinkable horror that stands against every significant principle of the faith. Yet throughout history, acts of genocide have been repeatedly justified (and sometimes celebrated as necessary) by those who, otherwise, are considered decent Christian men and women. The silence of the Christian churches in these instances implicates our community in the very process we profess to condemn.

The deliberate destruction of Native American communities by early settlers and the several following generations is a concrete example of a prolonged, systemic project of genocide involving both gradual as well as explicit measures. These first inhabitants of our country were forced from their land to inhabit environments that were completely foreign to them, killed in outright warfare and robbed of any assets that could sustain a flourishing way of life. All of this was done moreover, in the name of creating a "Christian" nation, "for the glory of God."

While the Middle Passage was a horrendous event on all fronts, conditions of extremely close quarters, inadequate ventilation, scarcity of adequately nutritious food, and lack of medical attention guaranteed that massive numbers of less abled captives would perish during the transit. In that way, the economic burden of caring for those who could not return a profit was lessened. Since sickly, or physically challenged blacks could be of little service, but would still require the expense of material resources, they were dispensable. An estimated fifteen percent of the two million potential slaves who left Africa died before reaching the shores of the New World.

In an article on colonial expansion onto Native American land, historian, L. Frank Baum, supported the idea of genocide by asserting that "Whites, by law of conquest, by justice of civilization, are masters of the American continent, and the best safety of the frontier settlements will be secured by the total annihilation of the few remaining Indians."[66] The horrible history of lynching of African Americans and others throughout almost one hundred years of American history is another example of a protracted campaign that involved the loss of more than 5000 African American men, women, and youth between 1882 and 1968.

---

[66]Baum, the editor of the *Aberdeen Saturday Pioneer* editor in South Dakota newspaper in the 1890's, and creator of the bestselling childhood fable, *The Wonderful Wizard of Oz,* was a proponent of killing every Native American in retaliation. This editorial appeared in the December 20, 1890 edition of the paper.

ITERATIONS OF WILL TO POWER

There are six things which the Lord hates, Yes, seven which are an an abomination to Him: Prov 6:16

If we are honest, we must find ourselves at some point on this continuum in relationship to some other or others. None of us is totally exempt, though hopefully, as Christians we fall or are moving toward the lower end of the scale. More hopefully, our recognition of our complicity in some form of the Will to Power pushes us to be always confronting our motivations. To always be wrestling with the realization that we are susceptible to the malady and struggling to overcome the sinful tendency lodged in us.

All iterations of the Will to Power have the potential of manifesting themselves within any one of the contexts in which we are juxtaposed against an other not completely like us. And since each of us is uniquely crafted by God, no one person completely like any other person. So, we are all, continually, challenged by this ever-present difference to either act out Kingdom principles or capitulate, in some way, to our baser proclivities toward othering. It is almost always easier and more convenient to capitulate, especially when so many opportunities are provided for us to do so. For capitulation, momentarily at least, reduces the stress of being seen as at odds with the perceived interest of our reference group. It saves us from having to defend treating the other with the dignity and respect they deserve as full participants in God-imaged humanity and the world that God so loved, when it is not the habit of our group to do so.

Each of these iterations – each of these isms potentially presents a paradox in they may, at the same time, be inconsequential and have heavy consequences. Some judgments regarding race, gender, class, sexual identity, age, abledness, national interest, religion, or economic status of the other are trivial and have little consequences for the quality of their daily existence or material welfare. Whether we invite them to be our friend, allow them to be vital members of our congregations, or move into our neighborhoods does seemingly little to change the essential fabric of their lives. Yet some judgments have far reaching implications, not only for the material well-being of a single other, but for entire communities, as well as for our sense of safety. Whether we judge the other to be a political or military threat or choose to share or withhold needed resources has the potential to become a matter of life—or death!

Much of the casual, or deliberate, judgments we make, however, have to do with our ignorance – our choice to ignore the very real, and inescapable truth of their lived experience. Deliberately unpacking these isms, brings us face to face with the reality of their experience. And, this unpacking is a first step in moving beyond the impasse in relation to the other.

Racist Will to Power

Racism is one of the most evident renditions of Will to Power within the current culture. The simplest definition of racism is discrimination or prejudice toward individuals or groups based solely, or primarily, on racial or ethnic identity. This discrimination assigns intrinsic value to the individual or group based on racial distinction. It begins with the simple premise that racial groups differ in their innate capacities and involves making personal judgments about an individual or group, in a variety of areas, based on these attributes. But it can also be a pervasive, systematic way for one entire racial group to deal with all members of an entire other racial group.

Assuredly, race is a social construct that could stand to be dismantled, while our true identity is lodged within our ethnicity. For many individuals, such ethnicity is an admixture going back through several generations of inter-cohabitation. Further, racism is not an American, or even a modern, construct. Vestiges of it have existed in some form in every society and every age. Racism is not an action. It begins as a prejudicial, discriminatory attitude toward the other based solely or primarily on their perceived racial identity. Yet, since black, brown or yellow people did not create the social climate that supports these racial ideations, it is naïve to expect that those who are oppressed by racialized systems can be responsible for dismantling them.

The least politically acceptable form of racism within contemporary, civilized society is overt racism, characterized by unconcealed hatred for and explicit discrimination against individuals based on their being a part of a specific racial or ethnic group. More, and more, however, the current political climate has supported, or at least justified, some manifestations of even these extreme attitudes and actions.

On the other hand, aversive racism implicitly involves employing unconscious negative evaluations of other racial or ethnic categories to persistently avoid interaction with members of those groups. This racism is more complex, as ambivalent expressions and attitudes involving subtle racialized behaviors are rationalized by appeal to rules or stereotypes. People can behave in an aversively racial manner while professing egalitarian beliefs. These same people will often deny any racial motivation for their behavior; while unconsciously changing that behavior when dealing with a member of a racialized group, and without being aware that such behavior can potentially have serious implications for the economic, political and legal welfare of the racialized group.

Color blindness purportedly disregards racial characteristics in social interaction, while, in fact, it refuses to attend to racial disparities within a culture. In doing so, racial color blindness, actually—though perhaps unintentionally—perpetuates patterns that produce racial inequality. Ostensibly color-blind racial attitudes and practices ignore race yet, at the same time, they subtly normalize the majority group's race. At an individual level, this type of racism rejects bigoted ideology, but, at the same time, rejects systemic remedies that could help dismantle institutional racism.

Since World War II, culturalism has emerged as a set of beliefs and customs that assumes that the products of a given culture, including its language, customs, moral standards, aesthetics, rituals, and traditions are superior to those of other cultures. Cultural racism involves a xenophobic understanding, often characterized by the fear of, or aggression toward, members of a targeted society that operates when widely accepted stereotypes about different ethnic groups and their culture are used as cues to determine the essence of their worth. Where racism characterizes one race is inherently superior or inferior to another, culturalism characterizes an entire culture—not just the racial group, but, all its consequent cultural elements—as inherently superior or inferior to another. One of the ugliest, most explicit forms of cultural racism has been exhibited in centuries of Western colonialism in the Americas, Africa, and Asia that, often, have been justified by white supremacist attitudes. During the early twentieth century, the myth of the "White Man's Burden," for example, served to justify imperialist policies as a noble enterprise for rescuing what were considered "lessor" cultures from their desperate state. When attitudes of black, Arab, or Asian supremacy exist, they deserve no more credence than this unfortunate position.

Historically, economic or social disparity has allegedly resulted from past discrimination in formal education or other preparation, denial of adequate health care, or failing to provide appropriate family support systems. These deficits continue to affect the contemporary generation through, primarily unconscious, racist attitudes and actions toward the subject population. During the Spanish colonial period, for example, Spaniards developed a complex racial caste system for determining and controlling a person's status in society. At the time of independence, many Latin American countries rendered the system illegal. Yet, residual racial prejudice based on perceived distance from European ancestry supports remnants of the colonial caste system.

Institutional, structural or systemic racism is carried out by governments, agencies, corporations, religious groups, or educational institutions who hold power to negatively affect important aspects of the lives of members of a minority group. In the late 1960s, activists, Stokely Carmichael coined the phrase institutional racism to mean "the collective failure of an organization to provide an appropriate and professional service to people because of their color, culture or ethnic origin."[67]

Racial discrimination simply refers to the partitioning of racially identified individuals or groups into categories that would not usually be related to race for purposes of differential treatment. Official or quasi-official racial policies may formalize these types of practices, but it is possible to exert them without any formal support. Candidates for employment, for example, who are perceived as having "white-sounding" names are often more likely than those whose names were merely perceived as "sounding black" to receive callbacks for interviews though no formal policy exists to support the practice. Or educational resources may be differently allocated based on some assumption that members of a racial minority do not have the intellectual acumen to take advantage of more appropriate materials. Such practices show compelling evidence of unconscious bias rooted

---

[67] Carmichael, a black nationalist and one of the leading figures of the Black Panther Party first used the term in 1967. See Stokely Carmichael and Charles V. Hamilton, *Black Power: The Politics of Liberation,* New York: Vintage Press, 1972, 4.

in a history of discrimination (e.g., Jim Crow laws, etc.) that has not been disavowed.

Racial segregation separates people into socially constructed racial groups for the carrying out of their daily lives. Though explicit forms of segregation are, now, generally outlawed, such practices may exist through social norms or historically institutionalized patterns, even when no strong individual preference for it exists.[68] Though, for example, segregated housing is statutorily outlawed in the United States, throughout the country, historic and economic realities have created patterns in which many, if not most, people live in communities where many, if not most, of their neighbors, are of the same race. Consequently, though segregated education facilities are no longer legally upheld, many, of the nation's public schools are still racially homogeneous or have a small number of students who are not members of a majority racial group. Further, though, in this country, fair employment opportunity is the law of the land, our work places and job patterns often reflect racial segregation. Within the corporate world, for example, decades of historic patterns of exclusion mean that it is still rare to see people of color at the head or higher ranks of corporate leadership or on boards of major corporations in any significant numbers.

Symbolic, or modern, racism is a subtle form of the malaise characterized by outwardly acting unprejudiced while inwardly maintaining prejudiced attitudes, displaying subtle prejudiced attitudes, behaviors or actions informed by attributing qualities to others based on racial stereotypes, and appraising the same or similar behaviors differently, based solely or primarily on the race of the person being evaluated.

Symbolic racism rests on the belief that people of the other race are morally inferior and violate traditional "higher" values of our group

[68]This is suggested by Thomas Schelling's models of segregation. See, for example, his *Micromotives and Macrobehavior,* Revised Edition. New York: W. W. Norton & Company, 2006.

– as the symbol of what we are not. It can be more generally characterized as an open derogation of individuals unlike ourselves who signify one or more cogent characteristic that is not like us—as a reminder of what we do not want to be.

Symbolic racism allows us to easily dismiss an entire group. For many black people, for example, whiteness, at its face, symbolizes privilege. The individual white person that we encounter and with whom we might have any level of difficulty epitomizes all that is wrong with "white people." It is difficult, therefore, for any genuine overture by individual white people to erase that symbol from the black psyche.

Some prejudiced people do not view symbolic racism as prejudice since it is not linked directly to race but indirectly to social and political issues the race represents. Much of the current socio-political and moral debate is clearly related to race but is coded in socially acceptable language that reveals the symbolic nature of racial attitudes. It is not that these other people are bad, but that they symbolize an infringement on our "rights," a derogation of "the American way" and all that is "good" about the country, and of all that has historically made this country "great."

This prejudice and discriminatory behavior allow individuals to act ambivalently toward another group, evidencing positive reactions in certain, public settings, but negative expressions in more private contexts. This ambivalence may be visible, for example, in hiring decisions where employers might positively evaluate highly qualified job candidates while unconsciously disfavoring them in the final decision because of race. Some scholars characterize modern racism as an explicit rejection of stereotypes, combined with resistance to changing any discriminatory structures for, ostensibly, non-racial reasons. They insist that opportunity is a purely individual happenstance, denying the relevance of race in determining that opportunity.

Sexist Will to Power

One of the most lingering and deepest iterations of Will to Power is exhibited in holding and acting on attitudes about a person and engaging them in a favorable, or disadvantaged, manner based solely on their gender. This rendition of the malady is almost as old as Creation itself. For, since the first couple's fall in the Garden of Eden, the much-noted "war between the sexes, has continued to be waged on many levels. Some men see the descriptive biblical passage that asserts that, "because you have done this…I will put enmity between [the man] and the woman,"[69] as prescriptive. The blame game began with the contention that, "The woman whom You gave to be with me… gave me from the tree, and I ate."[70] Since ancient times, many men who participate in the Will to Power have continued to cast women as the spoilers of all that is good—the temptress, the seducer.

While we generally understand sexism to relate to attitudes and actions men exercise against women, sexism can be employed by either gender. Yet, within contemporary culture, where men hold most of the power, we most often see sexism displayed in negative attitudes and actions against women that, somehow, relegate them to second-class status in which they are never afforded full moral agency, but are expected to fall in line with cultural expectations about their behavior.

Sexism exists at multiple levels. It may be interpersonal, familial, corporate, institutional, or societal. It may be unspoken or blatantly explicit. In the end, it becomes internalized and women begin to see themselves, as well as to relate to other women, as somehow problematic. They begin to view themselves as needing to conform to the pre-set expectations of their culture, even to the point of their own harm.

The extreme version of internalized sexism is the inner voice within the abused woman convincing her that, somehow, she is responsible for and deserves the treatment she receives. She persuades

---

[69]Gen 3:15

[70]Gen 3:12

herself that something she has done – some sin she has committed – has brought on this abusive behavior and that if she were to become more acceptable, things would change. Such self-blame leaves these women unable to speak up for themselves, even in the most extreme cases. Everyone except the abuser may become the perceived enemy so that genuinely dangerous cases go unreported for years, eventually leading to the death of the abused.

Internalized sexism causes women to adopt attitudes that limit their vision of what they can do or be and, relatedly, of what other women should do or be. It renders them incapable of articulating personal goals or strategically moving toward attaining any goals they may have. Women whose attitudes, actions or expectations fall outside these limits are considered to have stepped out of their place.

Conversely, spoken and unspoken ideas about what a "real man" is like locks some men out of opportunities to wholeheartedly pursue career or family aspirations that do not align themselves with cultural expectations. These men are forced to take on roles for which they may be physically, mentally or emotionally unsuited to present an acceptable public face of masculinity. They may be expected to "man up" and hide any genuine pain or emotion they might be feeling since any such expression might be considered feminine. They may be expected to adopt macho a façade that degrades women, so they can "fit in with the boys" in locker room talk. Sexual violence committed against men (by women or other men) does not receive the same scrutiny, outrage, or punishment as that same act against women. To assume otherwise—that sexism only involves inappropriate attitudes and actions toward women is to give in to the Will to Power, by negating the experience of men who are sometimes subjected to equally demeaning behavior.

Sexual harassment, the most blatant form of sexism, is a set of attitudes and actions that regard women solely as objects of erotic pleasure and treats them as if this were true. With it, women, it is felt, serve mainly to assuage the carnal appetites of men. While the most egregious forms of harassment may involve men physically acting out inappropriate behavior including rape or other unwanted contact; unwanted verbal overtures such as unseemly jesting, suggestions of inappropriate relationships or uninvited and unwanted advances can be equally demeaning and may come from persons of either gender.

Misogynist Will to Power

As uncomfortable as sexism may be, its devastating effects are no match for its more dastardly sister, misogyny—the deeply ingrained contempt for, or hatred of, women. In its most virulent aspects, misogyny is not simply debilitating or demeaning. It is physically, emotionally, mentally and spiritually deadly and takes away women's right to be fully human, leaving them in a state of perpetual fear for their wellbeing.

Sexism and misogyny can exist side by side. Yet while sexism may be personal or communal, misogyny is generally corporate. Entire societies participate in, support or tolerate misogynous practices. When women are subject to the imposition of sexism they are personally dehumanized, but when those attitudes result in physically or emotionally abusive behavior that is tolerated or ignored by the larger community, it is misogynous. Further, while sexism may be personally demoralizing, the consequences of misogyny are disastrously widespread. For, again, while sexism breeds personal attitudes and behaviors, misogyny breeds systems of oppression, that are upheld by the social structure.

Within misogynous cultures, this expression of Will to Power initially exhibits itself in narrow manifestations such as imposed dress codes, restrictions on education, or limitations on involvement in public activities such as driving, working outside the home, voting, or holding public office. In extreme forms, however, women are regularly subjected to such heinous behavior as gendercide or female infanticide, genital mutilation, sex trafficking, forced child marriage, honor killings, witch dunking, sati (widow burning), and sanctioned spousal abuse including beatings and rape.

Misogyny plays itself out in social exclusion, where women who dare insist on expressing their full humanity are subject to belittling, incarceration, hostility, or violence—including death. The most obvious outcome of this isolation is that individual women are made to feel that they have no recourse. Women who refuse to conform to misogynist systems must, ultimately, be destroyed for the sake of the community.

Misogyny locates the full authority of the society in patriarchal systems that operate on the pretext of preserving some higher moral ideal. Misogynous cultures view women, not just as different and weaker, but as purveyors of an evil that, in the least, must be contained, or ultimately, completely subjugated. Further, generally, only men are offered the opportunity to decide what that ideal is. Those who are most affected by these ideals and the practices used to support these ideals, usually have no voice in shaping them. Since these attitudes are ingrained within generations of misogynist practices and supported by religious, economic and social sanctions, they prove exceedingly difficult to dislodge.

Even within the twenty-first century, the global problem of misogyny has a greater impact than most people imagine. At the turn of the century, more girls were subject to gendercide than men were killed in all twentieth century military combat.[71] Sexual trafficking of young girls and women, which, until recently, many saw as a problem plaguing regressive societies, has taken on epidemic proportions within many, seemingly more progressive, cultures.

---

[71] Nicholas D. Kristof, and Sheryl WuDunn. *Half the Sky: Turning Oppression into Opportunity for Women Worldwide*. New York: Alfred A. Knopf, 2009.

Classist Will to Power

All things being equal, we assume that the failure of other individuals or communities to be as well off as our own is due solely to conditions they have brought on themselves and could control by applying the same discipline we, and our community, have applied. In the most modest expression of classism, we assume that they are not as ambitious, not as intellectually fit or not as self-controlled as we have been. In its most egregious form, however, we contend that they are lazy, stupid or in some way, immoral. Or conversely, if they stand in a higher social class, we contend that they are elitist and uncaring. In either case, we infer, with this assumption, that a reversal in one or all these dispositions would correct their situation. Yet, truthfully, all things are never equal. Material resources that support class privilege have been made available to us while kept out of the reach of the other.

Like most isms, classism can be manifested at both extremes. Two manifestations of classism – intellectual elitism and anti-intellectualism –graphically demonstrate this point. Intellectual elitism uses educational attainment as a badge of intelligence and merit for allocating certain resources (most notably economic) within a community. Not just that we are educated, but where we are educated and by whom, becomes a standard for judging suitability for undertaking a number of tasks – many of which have no real connection to one's educational attainment. Innate intelligence is disregarded as having little significance and common skills that are necessary for the support of the community are devalued. Those who have not obtained our requisite measure of education are, therefore, not considered as worthy conversation partners or capable of forwarding an adequate solution to issues.

Conversely, anti-intellectualism robs a community of resources that collaboration with other members can bring to it. Further, like most isms, anti-intellectualism exhibits itself in several ways. Assumptions are made that those who have attained a level of education only use it to take advantage for themselves. At first glance, such sentiment can seem to be the simple benign disregard for the contributions of the educated class. Throughout history, however, totalitarian regimes have considered those with education as a threat and targeted them as enemies with despotic projects – sometimes with dire consequences for the larger community.

Ironically, neither intellectual elitism, nor anti-intellectualism, have much to do with intelligence. Both are more aptly related to perceptions that obtaining or failing to obtain a prescribed level of education renders the individual as other. Often with unfortunate consequences, we proceed with notions about them and relate to them, based on that limited information. For we either automatically defer to them in areas where they have no knowledge, granting them too much voice in intellectual engagement or we give little credence as to what they can contribute to us. In either instance, little attention is paid to what they may genuinely bring to resolving the issue at hand.

Another example of classism, caste systems, rigidly lock entire groups of people in a multi-generational stratum that defines not only what they should expect to receive from the society in which they exist, but also what they are expected to provide for it, and how they are to relate to members of other castes within that society. Though existing within numerous cultures, the situation of East India readily comes to mind when we think about this rendition of Will to Power. The caste serves as a type of self-fulfilling prophecy, since expectations are set for individual members of each caste before birth. If the parents are poor, we assume their parents and grandparents were also poor. But, more importantly, we expect that the child, and their progeny, will be poor. There is no hope of transcending a system that has been set in stone by the accidental situation of one's birth.

While class is often tied to outwardly observable identifiers, seemingly it should be the easiest ism to break through. As difficult as they may be to obtain, we feel that remedies such as amassing wealth, procuring an education, or marrying should serve as vehicles for, at least partially, transcending class restrictions. Yet, for many, one can never fully escape their class identity or achieve a "higher" status when markers such as language, dialect or grammar, mode of dress or lack of shared history indicate to the powers that be, as well as remind the new arrival, that they have never fully arrived at the "higher tier" and, simply, do not fit.

Importantly, such class prejudice is not always openly verbalized or acted out. Rather, it is a tacit, unspoken indicator of how the other should be engaged. In these instances, class markers serve as silent cues about, sometimes, intangible or imperceptible ways we distance ourselves from the other. And such attitudes and actions have latent consequences for their wellbeing, since we may be prone to allocate material as well as psychic resource and accord differing levels of respect based on class perceptions.

Sexual Identity as Will to Power

The struggle over the subject of gender identity continually challenges the Christian community with its potential for radicalization by either side. Both sides claim to hold *the* biblical position and indicts the other as either being radically perverse or failing to accord full humanity to their perceived opponents. Both accuse the other of contravening Christian values and seek to silence the opposition in the public square, do away with legal remedies that appear to encroach on their position, or impose standards of public acceptance on what should be a very private matter. Their accusations, and counter accusations, are often loud, intense, and framed in language that is brutal, dispiriting, and insensitive.

Conviction of the rightness of a claimed biblical position does not, however, warrant misuse of Scripture as a weapon to devalue and vilify others. Further, there has not always been clarity, from either side, that the full measure of the Gospel is the proclamation of God's love and desire for reconciliation for all sinful humanity. Such failure forces those who see the gay and lesbian lifestyle as sinful to wrestle with how to hold a conviction of the sinfulness of a behavior without promoting hatred or denigrating those with whom they disagree. While the expression "hate the sin, but love the sinner" often appears trite and offhanded, progressive Evangelicals struggle with framing responses that denounce manifestations of sin while wholly embracing all sinners (including ourselves) as fully human persons deserving the respect of their God-imaged createdness.

Both sides struggle to justly live in relationship with those with whom they disagree without being required to endorse or reject lifestyles, promote or renounce practices or restructure qualifications for leadership within faith communities. Simultaneously, both grapple with refraining from vindictive rhetoric that dismisses the human dignity of those with whom we disagree and adopting more humane responses to the issues of homosexuality and gender identity.

Importantly, both camps grapple with refraining from making and reacting to pronouncements that apparently sanction behavior that brings harm to the other community. Such declarations create a lethal climate in which some secretly nurture a personal battle, while loudly hurling diatribes at others who openly insist on a God-given right to live out their identity and lifestyle. This struggle is evident in language or actions that tolerate, excuse, or condone uncivil, violent or inhumane treatment of gay, lesbian, bisexual or transgendered persons when we would never participate in such behavior ourselves.

The communication of the message of the universal possibility of redemption does not allow the Evangelical community to elevate homosexuality above other behaviors it considers sinful. For the fallenness that brings about other forms of sinful behavior is no less severe than the fallenness that displays itself in this behavior. Further, harsh invectives from either side do nothing to create or further God's intended intimate relationality.

Speaking from within the broader Evangelical community, Southern Baptist Theological Seminary president, R. Albert Mohler Jr.'s contention that, "[h]omosexuals are waiting to see if the... church has anything more to say after we declare that homosexuality is a sin" is sobering.[72] His words invite a clarifying voice from the Christian community. It is an invitation for the church to craft a compassionate response that seriously tackles the biblical insistence that a lifestyle lived out in sexual immorality is unacceptable while affirming that a hateful response to any segment of the human family is never acceptable. Such an invitation provides an opportunity for members of the Christian academy to assist the church in this important project, (though it must overcome historic —and contemporary—suspicions hindering rapprochement between the two camps). Such a response must clearly uphold the biblical assertion that every person created in the image of God is equally loved by God, and that the result of the Fall is a humanity that exhibits its fallenness in a plethora of ways.

The rightful desire of gay, lesbian, bisexual and transgendered persons to be treated with full human dignity as "created in the image of God" is legitimate. No perceived level of sinfulness removes any person either from that image or from God's love. Thus, no one can rightly insinuate that another person is unworthy of the love only God can offer, since no degree of fallenness can obliterate an image that is not imprinted on, but rather, is indelibly, ontologically and hieroglyphically embedded in the core of our very being. Our failure to discern that God-imaged createdness in the other derives from our own fallen, dim perception of its presence within those who are, in any significant way, unlike us. If Christ's atoning sacrifice was for all humankind, since all of humankind is fallen and requires redemption, we are always challenged to foster responses that point to genuine love for all, while defending what we perceive as the truth of God's word.

Still, the LGBT community does not get a bye in being able to use tactics that attempt to publicly disenfranchise those who are unable to wholeheartedly support their claims of the ethical and moral viability of their behavior. By the same token that homophobia renders

---

72Albert Mohler, No Truth without Love, No Love without Truth" Florida Baptist Witnessed http://gofbw.com/blog.asp?ID=10205, viewed January 30, 2010.

proponents of the gay lifestyle as unworthy of consideration, the tendency of heterophobes to render all who do not fully accept the gay lifestyle as unloving or unjust is equally untenable.

The conversation quickly shuts down when individuals within either community paint all people who disagree with their position as phobic. Certainly, for example, Evangelical Christians hold a variety of positions on the issue. An increasingly smaller minority, promote demeaning suggestions about how the LBGT community should be viewed and treated. While many others, see the gay and lesbian lifestyle as being outside of the bounds of biblical morality, they arduously affirm that persons within the LBGT community deserve the same human dignity and respect that is afforded to anyone else.

Further, a growing number of those within the broader Christian community (including some Evangelicals) strongly support access of those within the LGBT community to common civil rights, despite reservations about the behavior. Moreover, these same, more conservative, Christians are being forced to confront the reality that some within their circle of natural and church families, friends, and colleagues participate in this lifestyle. And this realization has brought with it a need to craft more generous responses that do not create chasms between themselves and those whom they love but with whose lifestyle they disagree.

The LGBT community cannot, therefore, loosely accuse all of those who do not hold their position as homophobic They may rightly, contend, however, that when heterosexist discrimination or prejudice deprives those within the LGBT community of basic human rights and relegates them to less than human status, it is a form of oppression. Homophobia is not simply holding the belief that the attendant lifestyle is not biblically acceptable. Instead, it is hatred, mistreatment or fear of LGBT persons simply as members of that community and targets their lifestyle as an unpardonable sin. It relegates the lifestyle of those within the LGBT community to a position of its own, beyond all other perceived sinful behavior. Those within this community are not viewed as individuals, but are lumped as part of a, supposed, agenda and collectively seen as a threat to all that is decent and sacred. There is no nuancing, and resultantly, there is name calling, bashing and vilifying of those within this community while sensing they deserve any treatment they receive. Further, when that attitude goes beyond that to become an irrational fear of, aversion to, the LGBT community it can be called homophobia.

Both homophobia and heterophobia exhibit themselves as an inability to hold authentic conversations with members of the opposing community. Both use denigrating language to speak of persons within the opposite camp. Both are, unfortunately, represented in counter accusations of agendas. The tendency to too quickly evoke either the terms "homophobia" or "perversion" immediately shuts down the conversation with anyone who does not acquiesce to our position.

For the sense, from those on both sides of the issue, is that there can be no compromise—it is an all or none issue. There can be no privately held convictions. One side loudly hurls accusations of damnable perversion, while the other retorts with vehement allegations that there is a prideful and damnable lack of love. There appears to be only two choices: call for the wrath of God to be visited on the other in dramatic Sodom and Gomorrah fashion, or call for the total absolution of any lifestyle the other chooses (as it often been alleged that Jesus would have done). Either of these solutions misses the mark. And so, there is a moral and spiritual impasse with no easy way forward on an issue that threatens to be one of the most divisive within modern Christian history.

Generational Will to Power

Generationalism encompasses socially constructed thinking about persons based on negative stereotypes regarding their age group; and the tendency to structure society, based on these judgments. These ways of thinking see those within various age groups as having little of relevance to say to each other. It also exhibits itself in practices designed to take advantage of the vulnerability of an individual or group because of perceived characteristics related to age.

The most visible form of the malady is ageism. The term, coined by sociologist, Robert Neil Butler, describes a set of prejudicial attitudes toward older people, old age, and the aging process; discriminatory practices against older people; and institutional practices and policies that perpetuate stereotypes about them.[73] Though historically many cultures have reserved a level of respect, or even veneration, for older persons, the contemporary emphasis on youth has seen a reversal in this tradition.

Though the elderly comprise the fastest growing segment of most Western societies, age prejudice is among the most socially "normalized" of any isms. And since the aging process carries easily recognizable markers, ageist practices take a variety of forms. Dangerous instances of ageism occur when, for instance, a medical professional or system decides to provide or withhold medical care based solely or primarily on a patients' age because they determine it would better used on a younger person. But seemingly benign ageism includes avoiding being around older people, not listening to them or dismissing what they say as inherently irrelevant. Generally attributing certain practices to older people as a group, is perhaps the simplest, least intrusive form of ageism. Benevolent ageism, however, condescendingly assigns protection or benefits to older people as we assume they need them, whether this is true, or they desire them.

While our society holds age-related employment discriminate to be illegal, such discrimination can be hard to prove. Several mitigating factors can easily be cited as a rationale for not employing persons who are older or for reserving certain categories of positions to younger people. These factors place the onus on elderly persons to demonstrate

---

[73]Robert Neil Butler, "Age-ism: Another Form of Bigotry." *The Gerontologist.* 9 4) (1969)., 243–246.

their worthiness for employment in arenas in which they would, if given an opportunity, prove themselves well suited.

Interestingly, as with internalized racism, older people themselves can be the most rigid in adopting ageist attitudes. They may choose to stay away from other older people or ascribe certain attitudes or behaviors to those within their own age group simply because they are advanced in years. Such ageism may express itself as a denigration of the worthiness of projects or ventures attempted by those in their age group, or a feeling that they should "get out of the way" of younger people, allowing no merit for individual adaptability.

While the admonition to "act one's age" may itself be a form of ageism, older self-loathing may express itself in seemingly innocuous actions. Older people may alter physical evidence of aging through unwarranted chemical or medical procedures or adopt modes of dress and change apparel to evoke a younger image. Or, they may take on "inappropriate" behavior such as indulging in abusive substances or interacting with potentially harmful people to appear to be younger. Moreover, these behaviors relate to the Will to Power as individual responses to exclusion from a part of the community for which older people desire inclusion.

Certainly, these ageist tendencies can apply to any stage of life, where individual difference is not considered. Generationalism can be practiced at either end of the spectrum for the tendency toward age related prejudice runs both ways and even catches people in the middle, pitting generations against each other.

Discrimination against older people finds its reverse in rigid attitudes older people may hold against those who are younger. This reversion ascribes negative behaviors and attitudes to them and expects them to live those out. Young people can be dismissed as unable to contribute anything of value to projects simply because they are young. Their ideas and critiques can be dismissed as uninformed or lacking wisdom based solely on their chronological age, without any attention to differing degrees of maturity or intellectual acumen, or without regard to the Christian value of respect for people of all ages. Ageist practices toward the young include attributing certain practices to them as a group, avoiding being around younger people, disregarding their input, or treating them as if they were, somehow, dangerous.

Though studies show that specific characteristics are generally exhibited by those within specific age groups, in the end, generationalism segments people into rigid categories that dispose us to treat their members as a monolith. We forget that these boundaries are not static. And, while such distinctions may be useful for marketing purposes, our tendency to frame our interaction with those within these groups robs us of opportunities for valuable encounters and relationships that could potentially enrich our lives.

Those in the middle find themselves at odds with both groups at either end. They dismiss the wisdom of age as well as the innovation of youth. So, ultimately, we find ourselves fragmented into a tiered age hierarchy in which we are forced to either learn completely from our own mistakes operate without the benefit of newly developed knowledge that could potentially enhance or save or physical, mental or emotional lives.

Ableist Will to Power

Often, one of the most visible indications of difference and vulnerability is the degree to which an individual is physically, emotionally, or mentally abled or impaired. Truthfully, however, each of us is, to some degree, disabled. Medical pronouncements notwithstanding, no one who is a partaker in fallen human nature is a perfect specimen of health. In these areas, while some disabilities may be more explicit and obvious than others, each of us carries within ourselves some limitation to our abledness.

Still, the tendency to power over those who are more visibly impacted by disability can sometimes express itself in ways that are not conscious of. We often assume, for instance, that if an individual is physically disabled they are also, in some manner, mentally or emotionally impaired or vice versa. So, we find ourselves treating those with a single impairment as if they were multiply disabled and without allowing them the opportunity or freedom to use other fully developed faculties to the greatest extent possible.

Most often, we exhibit ableist Will to Power by relegating those with an explicit disability to secondary roles in most contexts, assuming that any limitation they display precludes them from substantial roles.[74] Or conversely, in situations that might require some accommodation that disadvantages or inconveniences us in some way, we expect those who are differently abled to function at full capacity, without being granted necessary aid. We resent that they require special consideration that infringes on our level of comfort in any way. For their need infringes on our time, causes us to have to change priorities, or detracts from the aesthetic of our environment.

`Without openly verbalizing our sentiments, we are like Jesus' disciples, when he healed the man born blind. For, we are tempted to assign blame, wondering secretly, whose fault it is that the other is less than fully abled. We are prone to question what deficiency the parents contributed to the DNA, what preventable accident of birth, or life, brought this about. And it is difficult to see, the works of God displayed in the other,[75] since they do not fit the portrait of God we have created in our image.

Since they do not look like us and sound like us, and more importantly, since they do not look or sound as we envision a perfectly abled God, we find it difficult to recognize the inherent value of differently abled persons. We struggle to see them as men and women who are created in and fully carry the image of God as, ontologically, as the essence of who they are as human persons. And, therefore, we

---

[74]See Amos Yong, *Theology and Down Syndrome: Reimagining Disability in Late Modernity (Studies In Religion, Theology, and Disability)* Waco, TX: Baylor University Press, 2007.

[75]John 9:1-3.

negate the common human needs of the disabled person to experience love and acceptance and to be able to contribute their skills, talents, and abilities as well as to full express their experience of joy, loss, and grief. For our idolatrous image of God fails to make room for their seeming lack.

Moreover, their disability is a constant, uncomfortable reminder of our finitude and the fragility of our tentatively abled state. The reality that "there but for the grace of God go I, becomes more than a trite cliché and we are forced to reckon with the provisional nature of our situation. So, it is easier for us not to have them in front of us. It is less stressful to keep them out of sight. In this way, we can get on with or lives without having to confront the implications of the mirror that their disability holds up to us.

On the other hand, some pretend that the other's disability is no disability at all, or, at least, not as much of a disability as they contend. We assert that they are abler than they profess and are using their situation as opportunity to power over us. We resent that they desire to extract resources from the system that should be ours.

The existential experience of disability is humbling; it forces an individual to live within functional and social limitation and accommodate themselves to dependence on others for assistance. Yet it need not be humiliating or dehumanizing. To a degree, the tendency to dehumanize the disabled comes from a failure to understand the particular needs of individual persons living with specific disabilities and, as with all instances of Will to power, lump them into an undifferentiated mass.

In return, disability can become an occasion to operate within the Will to Power. It can be used as a weapon to exact more resources and concessions than are, genuinely, required. Understandably, differently abled persons must navigate a social and structural world created for and by "fully" abled people who are not always willing, to discern the genuine obstacles that disability imposes. And their lack of discernment offers occasions for their ableness to become a point of resentment or the other.

People with less visible disabilities can be resented solely because they outwardly appear to be healthy. Or repeated incidents of insensitivity from some in the abled community can bring the disabled person to a place where he or she views all more abled persons as uncaring. At that point, the most earnest, though sometimes miscued attempts to render assistance are rebuffed for any number of reasons. Their responses are not quick enough, they do too little or too much, they fail to focus on my real area of need, they are miscued and awkward.

So, in the end, we are left with a situation that is frustrating for both sides And we fail miserably at creating relationships of mutually that allow the works of God to be displayed within the individual and their disabled reality. As well, we miss the opportunity for the works of God to be manifested to the world through a portrait of God-centered mutuality. And we truncate the possibility of allowing the disabled person to fully discern their God-imaged createdness.

No degree of physical disfigurement, emotional or mental limitation or cognitive lack can mar that indelible image. Therefore, and our unwillingness to comprehend this image in the differently abled other restricts the ability of our Christian communities to reflect it to the world.

Nativist Will to Power

While we expect individuals to identify with the geo-social community around which their everyday lives are centered, hyper-nationalism can be one of the most heinous and dangerous forms of Will to Power within the global nuclearized reality in which we find ourselves. Such parochial aggression has historically been the root of rigid nativist priorities that cause us to hear of "wars and rumors of wars" and pit "nation against nation and kingdom against kingdom"[76] in an ongoing tension that has permeated every realm of human activity since almost the beginning of known time.

We have convinced ourselves that God loves our nation and hates everyone else, or that, at least he loves us more. While Scripture is clear that Christ died for all, and that God is not willing that any should perish,[77] we pride ourselves in always believing that if we should ever take up arms, God would be at the head of our army for we are, always, in the right and, always, protecting God's interest.

As with the notion of American exceptionalism, extreme nativists see their country and its culture as uniquely superior to all others. Their national interest are seen as worth preserving against all others, at all cost, and protecting—even to the point of war. At first glance, such a simplistic definition of these nativist tendencies may appear to be a somewhat naive over assessment of the state of things. But its inherent danger should never be underestimated.

At its foundation, radical nativism incorporates an idolatrous syncretism of spirituality and national interest—such that God and country become so intermingled in the hearts and minds of its purveyors, that they cannot be separately identified. To promote the benefit of one is understood as promoting the advantage of the other. The name of God—whether it be Yahweh, Jesus or Allah or any other —is invoked in every national ceremony and national symbols are vividly employed at every religious gathering.

For in the mind of the extreme nativists, the nation becomes the portal to God's Kingdom. To work on behalf of one is to work on behalf of the other. To fight on behalf of one is to fight on behalf of the other. Within this context, justification is found for every villainous defense – war crimes of every sort, abrogation of human rights, or genocide are used in the service of protecting national (and God's) interest.

---

[76] Matt 24:6-7

[77] 2 Ptr 3:9

Such sentiments cause faith communities to incorporate nationalist themes into their worship experience. National flags are displayed in pulpits next to—or in place of—the Christian flag, patriotic creeds are recited, and anthems are sung. Sermons are crafted that embrace patriotic agendas as if they were mandates from God. And for those who purportedly are non-religious, nationalism takes on a religious fervor of its own.

Within this mindset, the enemy is always just outside the wall ready to pounce. Every overture toward peace is to be considered with skepticism. More importantly, extreme nationalism holds our nation harmless such that we are always the innocent party. We are always deserving of God's favor. For we represent God's side.

As the, presumed, innocent party, we do not see ourselves as driven by any narrow self-interest, but solely by the desire to preserve the interest of the highest moral and ethical standards. Assuredly, such a presentation is a myth, but we have convinced ourselves that it is true, and we invent slogans, and anthems to remind ourselves that this is so.

Throughout human history, every nation that has at one point assumed a measure of global prominence has exhibited this tendency. Rome, Greece, Spain, Great Britain, Germany, and the United States. And until now, each of these has been the subject of the natural decline that is part of the cyclical historical process. In reality, every world power has had its period of ascendancy and decline. No nation maintains global prominence forever. Nations rise and though no amount of nationalistic fervor can prevent it, we hold to our nationalistic pretentions in the hope that we can forestall the inevitable.

So, extreme nativism inevitably leads to excessive militarism. The buildup of military might at the expense of human services is a most often response to the felt need to protect one's nation regardless of costs to its individual members. Humanitarian projects are neglected, necessary infrastructure is left to erode, and more significantly, sons and daughters are sacrificed on the altar of patriotism.

It is reasonable for a citizen of any country to exhibit a degree of national pride. Members of each nation—Americans, Canadians, Germans, Indians, Jamaicans, Brazilians, or Ghanaians (or any other country) should be proud of what their homeland has achieved and contributed to the flourishing of humankind and global progress. Yet, we are all part of the universal human family and all share in the stake of a future that will either be filled with global aggression and distrust or, filled with a level of peaceful co-existence and tolerance.

As Christians, then, our allegiance should first be to the God of the entire universe who is not partial to any nation, but who loves every member of every nation equally. Or just as there is only one human race in which we all are partakers, there is only one global human family whose shared future is dependent on us helping to forge solutions that no longer pit "nation against nation."

Religious Will to Power

Religious Will to Power serves as the foundation for spiritual elitism—even in relation to other Christians—in which we contend that our tradition (our brand of the faith) is somehow truer, more theologically sound than any other. Further, we consider the sins of the other as more despicable than any pec within our own selves. And so, we consider any spiritual connection they attempt to make with us as an impossible venture.

The central assertion of Evangelical Christian faith that Jesus Christ is the only way to salvation, cannot be dismissed. It must be taken seriously, and its implications must be lived out at every level of our personal reality. Yet, within a democratic society that professes freedom of religion, this assertion itself does not warrant denigrating other religious positions, nor denying the same freedom of religious expression to those who do not hold our truth claims.

This assertion does not attest to the superiority of Christians as individuals or indicate that any others who are created in God's image are, in some way, more deficient in divine attributes than Christians.

Though those who succumb to religious Will to Power, may proclaim such, it does not imply that professing Christians are superior to members of every other religious system. Rather, it affirms that, in Jesus Christ, they are heir to a transformative experience that renders then capable of authentically loving others.

We all share two contradictory qualities. Each of us is a soul born as a partaker in one inherently sinful nature and desperately in need of salvation. Because of the Fall, every person, no matter how civil he or she might appear, is flawed and capable of the most dastardly acts of inhumanity. All of us need the grace provided for in the atonement.

More positively, every human person was born with the potential for intimate fellowship with God. None is excluded from the offer of salvation. Every person created in God's image has a measure of all the qualities that such creation suggests. Each of us has the capacity to authentically love others and involve ourselves in altruistic relationship. Each of us has the possibility for a degree of intellectual attainment to be used in the service of God and the other.

Religious Will to Power gets played out as bigotry and intolerance that is as sinful as any other form of bigotry. It occurs at every level and is variously directed at those of other faiths as well as those of other traditions within our own religious family. It shows itself within the Christian tradition as excessive zealousness for any segment of our own tradition. It is the cause of schisms at every level of the church that has kept it from being the integrated and healthy body of Christ it is called to be.

The vehement assertion that salvation is by grace alone – and that this grace is offered through the atoning work of Jesus Christ for all – is an admission that nothing in us merits special attention from God. That grace is unmerited favor that none of us deserves. Yet, somehow, we sense that those who do not share our faith convictions are not only lost or unredeemed, they are less deserving of salvation or unredeemable. We demonize them, projecting on them the epitome of evil and ascribing malevolent intent to their every action. We wish their damnation since, we tell ourselves, they deserve it. And further, notwithstanding Jesus' assertion that, "it rains on the just and the unjust," we attribute every misfortune that befalls them as the judgment of God, to which we hold them notably worthy. It is one thing to affirm that Jesus is Lord and to ascribe worship only to him. It is another to see people from other religious traditions as somehow less deserving of God's grace and somehow more deserving of God's wrath. So, when we do this, we fail to accord to them the spiritual dignity due to them as individuals created in the image of God.

Since faith is a deeply held personal value, insisting on required openness to other viewpoints is fraught with difficult challenges. Assuredly, only God holds the whole truth, and only God has it entirely right. We are convinced, however, that we, of all people through all ages, come closest to understanding Ultimate Reality. So, we set out to silence the other and keep them from exposing us to their untruth.

Certainly, Christians appreciate the call to love other members of the body of Christ. And even when those members represent a distance strand of Christian faith, we accord them a level of toleration that, often reluctantly, admits that they may have something of spiritual significance to say to us or that God may have some use for them in the Kingdom project. But non-Christian others present a problem for us. We not only castigate them as heathens, for their failure to embrace the Christian faith. Often, they are dismissed as summarily less ethical, less moral and, more importantly, less deserving of God's grace. So, though we must admit that Scripture adamantly conveys that God so loved the entire world, in our consideration of them, we invariably insist that God's love for us is more intense.

Religious Will to Power is further lived out in a tendency to stratify sin. The temptation is to consider those whom we feel have sinned more than we have as not as worthy of salvation. We feel a sense of satisfaction when we can say, "I was a hater, but he was a murderer. My heart was full of lustful wantonness, but she committed adultery."

There must be one who is more a sinner and, therefore, less deserving of God's favor, mercy, and forgiveness than we are. Otherwise, how can we feel justified?

The history of the Christian church is replete with unchristian remedies for those who are deemed not to toe the line, those who threaten the spiritual power structure. In the name of Christ, we have killed for any variety of self-justifiable causes. The Crusades, the Inquisition, the witch hunts all bear witness to this unfortunate tendency to scapegoat our religious detractors. Even the Holocaust was tinged with Christian undertones of supposed superiority. For while no one wholeheartedly endorsed the Nazi plan for the extinction of the Jews, much of the Christian world turned a blind eye and a deaf ear to the plight of those who were being systematically exterminated. And even while Evangelical Christians today loudly pronounce their loyalty for the State of Israel, many of these same communities remained eerily silent as the Jewish community throughout Europe suffered unspeakable atrocities.

At the extreme, all isms—all manifestations of the Will to Power—lead to the possibility of the justification of genocide for a targeted group. Yet, while religious faith is the sphere that potentially could draw all of humankind together, it has often been a major culprit in promoting the destruction of entire communities of individuals who carry the image of God.

We must continue to ask ourselves, how did the entire civilized world stand by as six million Jewish men and women, and children were systematically eradicated. Further, we must question how an entire nation was able to loudly declare itself Christian while at the same time maintaining an inhuman system that attempted to annihilate the entire Native American society and that denied basic human dignity and brought about the destruction of hundreds of thousands of African Slaves. [78] In both instances, they convinced themselves that they were doing God's bidding: The first instance reflects an anti-Semitic tendency to hold the Jewish people, as a whole, responsible for and to recompense the death of Jesus. The other reflects an understanding that they were bringing genuine religion to a culture they considered entirely heathen and rescuing all its members from pagan idolatry. Both are graphic instances of religious Will to Power.

Economic Will to Power

Another prevalent expression of Will to Power is the economic dominance that people, institutions, cultures, and society who control wealth and means of production hold over those who have less access to these commodities. After all, we are relentlessly bombarded with reminders that "money is power." And though we offhandedly remark that, "the best things in life are free," and no value can be put on intangible measures of well-being such as happiness, quality relationships or peace of mind, we are always aware that most of what is needed for our physical, emotional, mental, and even spiritual sustenance come at a material cost. Further, we understand that most members of the human family are never in control of the economic systems that manipulate these resources or grant us access to these commodities.

Though Christian Scripture insists that the love of money is the root of all evil[79] – the root of every attitude or action that can be labeled Will to Power, money remains an essential commodity for carrying out human commerce. Scripture is also clear, however, that the appropriate use of money and material resources can accomplish much good.

Conversely, the more material resources we control, the more economic power is available to us – that is, the more additional material

---

[78]In *American Holocaust,* published by Oxford University Press in 1993, David Standards estimates that more than 30,000,000 slaves died while in captivity.

[79]I Tim 6:10

resources we can produce and amass. Yet, these resources and this currency are not limitless. And so, the battle begins. For, in order for some to gain control of these entities, some must lose and relinquish some of their supply.

Indeed, money is a neutral, utilitarian commodity that symbolizes the availability of material resources necessary to determine and sustain our quality of material life. For that quality is determined, in part, by the level of economic power we hold. The more economic power we control, the more material resources are available to us and the more material comfort we can enjoy.

Jesus never chided individuals for having or using money to take care of real human needs. Rather, Jesus chastised those who loved money more than people, who used money to control or bring harm to others, or who would do whatever was necessary to get it. Likewise, the Old Testament prophets did not upbraid those who had garnered wealth, but rather railed against those who garnered it at the expense of the welfare of others—whether the stranger or their own countrymen. Repeatedly, prophets such as Amos, Micah, Isaiah, and Jeremiah protested the exploitation of their countrymen and women, as well as the stranger, for narrow economic motivations.[80] If it were only the lure of wealth, that would be one thing. But, it also involves the length to which some will go to extract wealth from the other or at the other's expense.

Historically, self-centered amassing of economic power has been implicated in a variety of instances of exploitation. Entire systems have been invented and maintained that, at their heart, have the exploitation of individuals or entire communities for the economic enhancement of another group. Medieval feudalism, American slavery, caste systems, and the practice of paying less than living wages all supported economic structures in which the few stood to gain at the expense of the many.

---

[80]See for example, Amos 5, Isaiah 1; and 58; Jeremiah 22; and Micah 6.

Systems are put into place: unfair labor schemes are established and supported by unjust laws, discriminatory practices relegate the other to low paying jobs, tax structures penalize the poor and benefit the wealthy. Religious, governmental and legal sanctions are employed to rob from the poor for the benefit of the rich. It is as if Jesus' declaration that "the poor you will always have with you,"[81] was a prescription for the treatment of those in need, rather than an apt description of the fallen human condition. For this admonition is often cited as justification for doing nothing to relieve economic injustice.

While it may be unreasonable to expect those who enjoy economic privilege to surrender any amount of that privilege on behalf of those who lack, such a project does not call for the destruction of any individual or group. Rather it promotes a Kingdom paradigm among those within the Christian community in which

> *all those who... believe [can come] together and [share] all things in common... as any [of them] might have need.*[82]

For some, any attempt such as this to bring about economic equity is viewed in determinately unflattering terms. Characterizations such as radical, heretical or unbiblical seek to deter all but the most determined from pursuing a remedy. Diatribes that bring about no resolution to the matter and only add to the existing divide are hurled from either side

Baptizing any economic system, be it capitalism, socialism, or Marxism as the biblical standard is heretical. Jesus was neither a political figure nor an economist. Neither he nor the prophets attacked any specific form of economic distribution. And neither did they prescribe any particular system. For they understood intrinsically that all humanly devised systems are not only flawed, but have the capacity to become demonic and to be used for exploitation. Yet, for Christians,

---

[81]Matt 26:11; Mk 14:7; Jn 12:8

[82]Acts 2:44-45

economic injustice is not a political issue. It is a biblical— Kingdom— issue.

Legends are invented about the scarcity of economic resources and the attempt of the other to extract them for us as we build ever bigger barns to hoard them away. Fear mongers paint pictures of dire time and admonish us to look out for ourselves and to protect ourselves from the coming onslaught at the expense of my brothers and sisters, and especially those who are not like us.

For, after all, priorities must be set. Those scarce resources must be allocated in a manner that does not privilege the other at our expense. Though we have more than enough for several generations, we cannot allow them to rob us of the security for which we have worked so hard, even if it has been at their expense.

Multi-Otherism

As traumatic as each of the isms may singularly be, the reality is that, generally, most of us are subject to or benefit from the intersection of several modes of othering. The harshest rendition of the Will to Power comes into play when two or more of these isms intersect to more rigidly undermine full human flourishing and God's intended relational intimacy among us.

Numerous examples of such intersectionality are present within our culture. Young, black men, for instance, carry the burden of age, race, and gender in attempting to navigate the realities of a contemporary society where many see them as exhibiting the foolishness of youth, the felt dysfunction of blackness and the aggression of their maleness. These interrelated realities often leave them in the tenuous position of having to defend themselves against several antagonistic audiences each with their working out of Will to Power over them.

Conversely, white, economically stable males are assumed to be racist because of their whiteness, sexist because of their gender, and oppressors because of their economic status. And while white men, by default, do benefit from the reality that they are male and white, in the eyes of some, there is never enough that they can attempt to do to redeem themselves. Every overture is considered false, simply because they are white, and male, and economically well-off.

This carnal, worldly mindset in relation to the other, leaves us unable to imagine the possibility that one could love us simply because we are what we are. It also leaves us at a place where they could not be worthy of our love due to the labels they carry. Every attempt to foster authentic relationship is greeted with a degree of suspicion and questioning what is in it for them. To do otherwise is considered naïve.

We consider any effort by the other to assist or embrace us in any way, it must be out of guilt, for we have declared them guilty. Or, we determine that they are acting out of need, for we have decided that they are deficient on several levels. We offer them no benefit of the doubt that their actions might be authentically grounded in an attempt to traverse the chasm created by the Will to Power, for we ourselves would never think to do that.

And at any rate, if they succeed in making overtures in one area, we do not give them credit for advances in the other. So, for instance, should a white man give up all his economic power, take a low paying job to work with economically challenged families headed by single mothers in the inner city, we would still never trust his motivations. For he is, still, male, and he is, still, white. We would tend to ascribe unflattering motivation to him which makes this always a lose-lose situation. And when, having failed to make inroads and gain trust, he might give up and walk away, we conclude that he was never sincere about what he was doing.

COMMON ROOTS OF THE WILL TO POWER

What is the source of quarrels and conflicts among you? Is not the source your pleasures that wage war in your members? Js 4:1

If we are honest with ourselves, at some point, we must come to terms with the reality that a measure of the Will to Power lies within each of us. We must ask ourselves, how are we at a place where no one can thoroughly trust anyone else, where no one can do as King suggested and, actually, get along and be at ease with the other beyond the surface level?

At their source, all manifestations of the Will to Power have a common spiritual core that is the outworking of our fallen human nature. To say that we are all victims of that fallen nature does not go far enough, however, in helping us unravel the threads of the puzzle of what is driving us so far away from each other.

Drawing on the discipline of sociology helps illuminate the multi-dimensional aspects and practical conditions that foster the flowering of the Will to Power within its various contexts. No single factor determines the depth to which we participate in it. We are always creatures of our inherited traits, the (productive as well as dysfunctional) nurture we receive within our communities, and the surrounding environment that shapes our view of reality. These inescapable influences are determinant in which iteration(s) of the Will to Power are most attractive to us and in which we operate most fluidly and frequently. Socialization, then, is a beginning point for how Will to Power comes to be in us. But it is augmented by our felt need to conform to the expectations our group has instilled in us so that we can protect us from all that is negative about the other.

The genuine oppression we experience from the other group reinforces what we have been taught about them and leaves us needing to be in control of our situation and our interaction with others. Yet, such perceived control, which evidences itself as an authoritarian personality, is really born out of deep insecurity and fear that we have no control at all, or at least, cannot control the most important things. And so, we must find a scapegoat to blame for this lack and restore our sense of security. And it is them!

Socialization

At its base, the ontological dysfunction of our fallenness is always and forever augmented by the ongoing process that occurs within the everyday interactions that begin in early childhood and continue throughout our lives. These make up the fabric of our communities of reference that allow us to acquire values and attitudes regarding those around us as we participate in significant social interactions that shape how we view and cope with the outside world.

We do not come to know the other on our own. Messages about them are always around us. We may not know exactly how, but early in our lives, we come to know that they are different and that our group is not entirely comfortable with them.

Almost from the moment of birth, we are given formal cues about how to navigate a reality filled with otherness. "Keep away from strangers," we are told. And we are warned to act in a certain manner in public, no matter how we are allowed to act in our own private places, so that they will not see our flaws or weaknesses and they will respect us.

Yet the informal, unspoken cues are equally, if not more, powerful. Gestures and unspoken attitudes play out in each encounter with the other. Inflections, tone of voice, what is said and not said about them, the giving or withholding of recognition, the willingness or failure to look them in the eye all tell us something about the other. And through them, we come to learn who they are and who they are to us. If they are friend or foe. If they are to be valued or devalued.

Narratives and myths about the other, handed down through generations, circle around us, get repeated in our hearing and take on a life and truth of their own. Ways of communicating with the other, as well as about the other, are repeatedly demonstrated by our parents and siblings, other family members, friends and members of our faith community.

But the cues are not just about them. They are also about how we are to react to, and interact with, them. These cues become our teachers as expectations are verbalized about how we should view and interact with them. When we violate these expectations, we are reminded of our inappropriateness.

For, in a recurring cycle, prophecies become self-fulfilling as the other reacts to our reaction to them. And their reaction confirms our socially formed suppositions about who they are and what they are about.

Conforming Behavior

As persons created for intimate relationality, we are social beings who long for the support of members of our group. We crave affirmation within our circle. Yet, access to that support and affirmation requires something from us. For the sake of all of its members, we must demonstrate our allegiance to the causes our community holds dear or we are subject to a degree of alienation.

Even when we think to ourselves or are convinced that the dominant attitude about the other may be dysfunctional, or even, sinful, we dare not challenge it too fervently. Since we desire acceptance within our own group, much of our professed notions, about the other are guided by groupthink (even when we secretly hold other ideas). For we are continually reminded that we must stick together and must think alike for the survival of the group.

As social beings, it is psychically easier to conform to our group's attitude toward the other – to go along with the dominant tenor of the masses about the other – to not make waves or cause dissonance. The treasonous act of siding with the other—seeing the reasonableness of their point of view—is intolerable. No acceptable justification for that view can be rendered, for such an open attitude is considered untenable.

In the present political climate, for example, any African American who declares themselves to be a Republican is, based solely on that decision, considered to be a sellout by many fellow African Americans. For those who hold strong political persuasions, no conceivable rationale for this choice is honorable and every argument to the contrary is considered bogus.

Though we may intrinsically know better, we are challenged, for the welfare and the good of group cohesion, to remain mute when negative stereotypes, derogatory caricatures, sexual innuendo, or racial or ethnic slurs are tendered. We laugh at jokes that are not funny and are demeaning or we pretend not to hear when an honest reprimand might be in order. In essence, we negate the needs of the other to secure a level of comfort equal to ours, though we might experience psychic and spiritual distress for our cowardice.

On the other hand, the other may sense a need to conform to expected norms because of an internalized Will to Power over them. For it is sometimes easier for the other to give in to the Will to Power over them than to fight a seemingly useless battle to extricate themselves. They sense that they cannot chance being subjected to a harsher dose of Will to Power should they fail to acquiesce. A person who is being cheated out of fair wages, for example, may "freely" decide to remain on a job, fearing they will be unable to find another.

Or they may stay, against their own wishes, if they sense that their financial contribution is required to make their group economically whole.

Experienced Oppression

The reality of subjugation has far-reaching implications for an individual's or group's ability to function productively in their context as well as to relate to the perceived oppressive group in any meaningful way.[83] Assuredly, the psychological trauma rooted in such subjugation is an inescapable part of the ongoing working out of Will to Power.

Whole systems are built on the premise that for one group to thrive, another group has to surrender something of significance—material and economic resources, spiritual, psychic or emotional freedom, or their natural way of life. The seeming reality that in order for one group to thrive, the other group must experience some type of loss or severe exploitation is part and parcel of the structure of social and economic systems. This idea, then, becomes taken for granted, without critical examination from those who benefit from it. For they surmise that this is the way things always have been, and therefore, this is the way things should be.

Yet years, decades and even centuries of such subjugation exact a toll from the exploited and the exploiter as well. No one goes unscathed, though some scars are more visible, and some wounds are more painful than others.

In her work, *Post Traumatic Slave Syndrome: America's Legacy of Enduring Injury and Healing,*[84] for example, Joy DeGruy lays out the protracted effects the slavery experience has wreaked on the collective

---

[83]For a deeper conversation regarding the reality of experienced oppression, see Muzafer Sherif, *In Common Predicament: Social Psychology of Intergroup Conflict and Cooperation*. Boston: Houghton Mifflin Company, 1966. pp. 24–61.

[84]Joy DeGruy, *Post Traumatic Slave Syndrome: America's Legacy of Enduring Injury and Healing*. Portland OR: Uptone Press, 2005.

psyche of African American people. DeGruy lays out the phenomenon of "vacant esteem" displayed in feelings of hopelessness, depression and a general self-destructive outlook, a propensity for anger and violence, extreme feelings of suspicion and perceived negative motivations of others as well as the internalized racism and self-loathing that leads to violence against self, property, and members of one's own group.

What DeGruy posits for the African American community, can be generalized to any oppressed community with the severity of the dysfunction, understandably being congruent with the length and severity of the subjugation. We should not be surprised, then, when members of oppressed communities exhibit learned Helplessness, a distorted self-concept, aversion for members of our own group, as well as for that of the oppressor.

Given that entire communities are often targeted for oppression (the slaughter of Native Americans, the American slave trade and Jim Crow policies, the Holocaust, repeated tribal and cultural massacres throughout the two-thirds world, as examples), entire communities suffer the prolonged dysfunction that accrues from it. This collective dysfunction drives a community to Will to Power as they seek not only to extricate themselves from the oppression, but to create a buffer between themselves and their oppressors, as well as to exact retribution. This is the only way they know to protect themselves from what they perceive as the danger of re-subjugation. Once extricated, moreover, they are prone to cast those oppressors and their progeny as perpetual enemies.

Authoritarian Personality

While as a group, all of humankind is subject to Will to Power, and no one is immune to it, some individuals who gravitate to the opportunity to dominate some other(s) in some way(s). The adrenalin rush of controlling the lives and fates of others is too much for them to resist. They must be in charge of someone, whether within a small arena or on a global scale.

People with authoritarian personalities are predisposed to exhibit the Will to Power. Commonly, authoritarians hold rigid beliefs, possess values that are less progressive than those of those in the mainstream of society, are generally suspicious of others, believe in a strict system of punishments, and are highly respectful of authority. They do not tolerate weakness in themselves or others. Their strong desire for conformity to social norms leads those with these personalities to gather around like-minded people while fearing the diversity represented by others and having anxieties about them.

Therefore, those within the white community with an elevated level of authoritarianism are often prejudiced against all minorities—people of color, Jewish persons, or immigrants are all problematic. Yet those with a high level of authoritarianism within any of these other communities will often also be quick to demonstrate prejudice against white people and anyone else who is not like them.

One of the most salient characteristics of these individuals is their propensity for absoluteness. As they see themselves, they are unequivocally right about the deficiencies and dysfunction of the other. And they require both an absolute measure of distance and the deference they are convinced they deserve from the other. No amount of information, no amount of positive interaction, can convince that they may, perhaps, be wrong.

The authoritarian personality is the true bigot. They can mentally and verbally condone all types of mistreatment the other, from inconvenient slights to egregious atrocities. For in their estimation, the targeted other has somehow brought such treatment on themselves. Their sympathy is always with the perpetrator, who they see somehow deserving vindication for some supposed wrong acted out against them. These individuals are among the loudest in repudiating others. They are not the vocal in supporting causes that stir up communal tensions, but in encouraging likeminded people to hold and act on these same attitudes as well.

Fear

Though seemingly bold, much of the invective of the authoritarian personality is driven by anxiety. For, the thing they crave the most, and the one thing they are most anxious is about not actually being able fully to protect their own possible descendancy or to control the potential future ascendancy of the other. The raw perception that the other poses a danger to some part of our wellbeing from which we need to be protected – leads us to act and react in ways that often do not line up with any rational understanding of the situation or person(s) confronting us.

A level of fear is a natural human reaction to the ever-changing contemporary world, where technology regularly confronts us with an enormous amount of potentially traumatizing disinformation. Yet even genuine, limited, fear can loom as enormous as we are continually bombarded with negative reminders of how dangerous our situation is. Since we can only process a limited amount of disruptive change in a short period of time without experiencing increasing anxiety, we become suspicious of everything and everyone. For we are repeatedly reminded that no one is to be fully trusted, and that to do so would be foolish.

Fear is both taught and learned. We are continually and increasingly taught to fear through cues provided to us through cultural engagement.

Fear is manipulated to boost media ratings, bolster political agendas, or sell products. These strategies cause distress about the changing social order that is not precipitated by a specific concern, but rather by a general sense that things are getting out of hand—that we are losing, and they are winning. Rhetoric is used to activate people's anxiety around a perceived threat from the other as a key to generating a positive response toward the "product" being sold. Our response to those cues, however, speaks as much about our valuing or devaluing the other and discomfort with the unknown as about our appreciation for the product.

As a major driving force in promoting the Will to Power, much of that fear comes from not venturing out to encounter that unknown in any significant way—not critically examining our encounters to either prove or debunk unfounded myths. And never getting to know the other at any less than a surface, artificial level, we continue to fear them.

Such anticipatory fear projects negative reactions toward a group even when we have never encountered any of its members. We hear repeated conversations about "them," they, or "those people," ascribing all manner of negative characteristics, attitudes, and actions to individuals whom we may never have had (and possibly never will have) occasion to encounter.

In a traumatized society where we are, relentlessly, bombarded by media with messages of the imminent threat of nuclear war, repeated economic upheavals, increase mobility, and relentless family distress, many are left in a state which we might rightfully characterize as Present Traumatic Stress Disorder. And, the level of ongoing stress is as real to us as any Post Traumatic Stress Syndrome experienced by veterans of war. We are always on heightened alert and always ready to respond in kind to any perceived threat to our physical, emotional or spiritual well-being—no matter how slight.

We learn to fear because of traumatic encounters with a group or any of its members that leaves us apprehensive of any further interaction with them. It may be a single encounter that we translate through already taught cues, but it is enough to convince us that we were right about them. Additionally, such traumatic encounters only reinforce and enlarge the fear that we have been taught to further ingrain it in our psyche.

We allow fear to become a constant state of anxiety toward them. We worry about what they would do to us given a chance, we worry about what they will exact from us. We worry that they may get the upper hand in any transaction we might undertake with them. And this fear generates one of four reactions toward the other.

We freeze in place and though we do not do anything to harm them, we do nothing to aid them, pretending that their cause is not real or that it is totally unimportant. We fight them with either using vilifying words that discredit everything they attempt to do, withholding resources, or by going to war. We flee from them by making every effort not to get close to them or taking steps to get as far away from them as possible. If they live in the city, we move to the suburbs, if suburbs become too concentrated with them, we gentrify the city and reclaim it as our territory. Or we build, figurative or literal wall to keep them out of our space and out of our sight. These walls are the variety of barriers we put up to keep them from opportunities for a good education, keep them out of well-paying, satisfying jobs, keep them out of neighborhoods, and out of our congregations. And we certainly keep them from ever breaking through the barriers that have become ceilings of achievement.

Taken together, our socialization, our tendency to conforming behavior, authoritarian attitudes, exposure to oppression, scapegoating, and fear encourage us to draw boundaries and construct identities to protect our group and "way of life" at all costs. So, we continue to build figurative – and literal – walls that keep *them* out and divide us from the rest of humanity as if, somehow, their flourishing could only come at our expense.

Scapegoating

The authoritarian personality finds a natural audience for his or her rants among those group members who need a reason for their failure to thrive or to make significant progress without implicating their own deficiency. In this exhibition of the root of the Will to Power, blaming the other for any problem or discomfort we experience displaces frustrated hostilities that could be produced by circumstances that cannot be easily explained or ameliorated.

Scapegoating comes about in one of at least two ways. Either we blame the target for any misfortune that happens to us either by dent of natural causes, cycles of history or our participation in our own fallenness. We know that bad things don't only happen to bad people, for as Scripture insists, "it rains on the just and unjust."[85] All of us are subject to the misfortunes of life. And though we understand this truth, at some level, we need someone to denounce – some culprit or fall guy – for any of our unfortunate, unexplainable or unresolvable situations.

Or, when we are a victim of any misfortune arising from an identifiable outside source but do not feel safe in voicing our displeasure at that source, we must vent our distress on someone. When subjected to the Will to Power over us, scapegoating allows us to deflect aggressive feelings away from an oppressor or enemy so as to not further endanger our wellbeing. While we cannot lash out at the responsible party without incurring harsh reprisal, we may safely redirect hostility toward more vulnerable others who have no control over, nor anything to do with, the situation.

Though the scapegoat is either innocent and has done nothing to deserve or is only minimally complicit in the situation, lashing out at him or her and heaping the full weight of blame on them is as a more accessible is a safer option than directly confronting the source of the discomfort. The recipe for effective scapegoating is to identify the most vulnerable targets: those who are outnumbered, already marginalized, or physically or psychologically weaker such that our tactics can further devalue them.

Scapegoating provides us with temporary, psychic relief, by assuring us, at a superficial level, that there is nothing wrong with us. This tactic helps us maintain the delusion that we still are in charge of

---

[85]Matt 5:45

our situation. Yet it is not spiritually satisfying, since, on a deeper level, we know that neither of these delusions is true.

Some part of each of these roots lies within every one of us. Moreover, each, singly, is powerful enough to breed some visible demonstration of the Will to Power. Each of us, however, – no matter how innocent we maintain we are – is subject to some amalgamation of these. And, further, since their combined presence is so integrally entwined, we find it all but impossible to extricate ourselves.

We can recognize its manifestations for what they are in ourselves as well as in those with whom we collaborate, or those who conspire against us. We can, then, acknowledge our complicity in holding and acting out these attitudes. And, finally, we can become genuinely repentant for the part we play, or have played, in its continued disruptive presence in the life of our communities, our communities of faith and our world. Only then, are we working to apply the correctives to dismantle the Will to Power, where we can, and ameliorate its effects where it cannot be dismantled.

A CORRECTIVE TO THE WILL TO POWER

"For all have sinned and fall short of the glory of God" Rom 3:23

God created humankind in God's image so that we would reflect the relational harmony of the Godhead throughout the created order. God intended that the essential harmony within the perichoretic Trinity would be passed on to that order such that members of the human family would not only "get along," but share in a distinctive unity with God and each other. The objective was to draw all of humankind into covenant intimate relationality that would find expression in deep appreciation for our collective experience. Sin, at its root, then, is any attitude or action that interrupts God's intended intimate relationality. Any attitude or action that, implicitly, or explicitly, disrupts that intention is evil and aligned with life-destroying darkness.

The New Testament vision of the church as Christ's body in which members endeavor to live out an atmosphere of unifying faith should move believers toward Christian maturity and vigilant participation in bringing about God's purpose. Fulfillment of this vision communicates the holistic salvific message to the world that God so loved. Even as Christians, however, our fallenness often places us at cross purposes with God's project, as we seek to protect our narrow self-interest at the expense of building community.

Like an insidious weed, never destroyed at its root, the Will to Power stealthily grows just under the topsoil of our human brokenness and alienation. It is fed by unfortunate misconceptions and experiences of the other and watered by the realities of life lived in constant stress mode. So, just as we think we have stomped it out with topical, short-lived applications, it returns in the surprising places where we drop our ethical vigilance and fail to discern our vulnerability. Just when we think we have eradicated all vestiges of prejudice, we are introduced to a new situation that throws us for a loop. Just as we begin believing we are delivered from discriminating, we are confronted by another whom we have not previously engaged, and the consciousness of the depth of our depravity hits us in the face.

Initially, like that sprouting weed, the Will to Power shows up in hard to perceive, seemingly harmless, ways—a distrust that simply keeps us away from the other or an uncomfortably demeaning, yet unspoken attitude toward them. Left unchecked, it grows and becomes ever more menacing. Simple distrust becomes fear as we discover reasons to move farther away from them. Fear becomes loathing as we verbalize the names we have invented to remind us and them of their inferior nature: "They" and "them, "boy," "girl," "nigger" "spic," "fag," "coon," redneck." Like the proud Pharisee in Scripture, we thank God that we are not like them [86] or as in the Jewish proverb that we were "not born one of them" instead of realizing that we, like all of them, require God's mercy.[87]

Artificial therapies do not eradicate the Will to Power from our soul. Legal recourse, education, nor integration change human hearts. Spiritual maladies require spiritual remedy. Under situations of extreme duress – war, pestilence, or economic downturn, even those least prone to operate within the Will to Power become susceptible. For it seductively pulls us into its embrace, offering the opportunity to experience ourselves as someone of worth—even while we are

---

[86]Lk 18:11

[87]Lk 18:13

convinced that we are not. The need to consider ourselves more, in some way, than at least one other is overwhelming. For it mistakenly convinces us that at least one person is more sinful than we are. We can be falsely assured that at least one person is less deserving of God's grace—as if unmerited favor is a commodity that can be earned. What is most unfortunate is that the false valuing of ourselves is a poor caricature of the true value that accrues to us as part of our indelible God-imaged createdness.

Yet, the Will to Power is too deeply ingrained in the human soul and psyche to ever be completely eradicated. Everything around us supports its development. Never having fully engaged or intimately known a single member of their community, we are bombarded with cues about how we are right about them, and that our suspicions are on point. We have never had an intimate conversation with a member of the group and know them only from contrived arenas imposed on us through work, the classroom, or business arrangements. What we know of them, therefore would be inadmissible as evidence in a court of law.

Still, the Will to Power continues unabated until the unfolding of the not-yet Kingdom. For the full restoration of God's intended intimate relationality will only come with the culmination of that Kingdom at the end of the age. Such a scenario might, on face value, sound hopeless for those who live in the present. Yet, the Kingdom has already come, in us. And this provides the opportunity to reflect its potential in places where it has not yet been realized. We are already to be active representations of what the not-yet Kingdom will be. And we are tasked with the project of strategically insinuating that Kingdom and its intimate relationality into every arena we touch.

Constraining the Will to Power

The lingering effects of debilitating syndromes must be managed so they do not destroy us. The Will to Power is such a disease. Like death, it is a consequence of our identity as fallen human beings.

Nothing we do can immunize us against it and no remedy has been found for it. It is part of our inherent sin nature. Lessening the effects of entrenched Will to Power, to any degree, involves deliberate, but necessary steps. We start by recognizing its real and powerful existence. Then we acknowledge our role in perpetuating the Will to Power by either actively supporting it or failing to call it out when we see it. And, finally, we commit to living in a state of perpetual repentance that resists the temptation to render that support and allows room for seeking authentic relationship with the other. For only then, can we effectively oppose the Will to Power. To miss any of these steps or attempt to put one before the other is to derail the entire project.

Recognition

Seeing the Will to Power for what it is becomes the first step in managing it. For, like an incurable disease with debilitating symptoms, denying its existence accomplishes nothing and, in the end, proves harmful. Like the symptoms of that undiagnosed disease, we are left feeling less than healthy but not knowing exactly why. We do not know, for example why we hate a certain group. All we know is that our parents did not like or trust them, and they taught us not to like them or trust them. We do not even remember what it is that we dislike or distrust about them. Often, again, we have never held a substantial conversation with any group member. So, we could not actually explain what we have against them.

In their excellent book, *How to Think Theologically*, Howard Stone and James Duke discuss the difference between holding an embedded theology handed down to us through our various traditions and developing our own thought-out, deliberate theology. These authors contend that each person holds a theological position which they demonstrate through their attitudes and actions, whether they are conscious of their assumptions or not.[88]

---

[88]Howard W Stone and James O Duke, *How to Think Theologically*, Minneapolis: Fortress Press, 1996.

This same contention can be made for the Will to Power. We are continually cued about how we should relate to our world and those who stand in various positions in relation to us. Every clue within our cultural matrix contributes to our attitude about those others. The family into which we are born, the institutions that educate us, the religious traditions, denominations, and local congregations that inform us and form us spiritually and ethically, the breadth and depth of our exposure to messages from media, as well as, our own experiences with people who are different contribute to the shaping of our attitudes. Often these attitudes are formed with little effort, as we passively listen and observe the postures, conversation, and actions of those who, explicitly or implicitly, form and nurture us. Through repeated exposure to these cues, we imbibe their world view and, at least partly, adopt it as our own. It becomes a part of our embedded theology about how to navigate interactions with the other.

Nonetheless, as we mature, begin to reflect on our stances, and are exposed to other possibilities for engaging others, navigating relationships becomes more complicated. When simple, habitual reactions become less spiritually satisfying, we are forced to recognize we are, possibly, wrong about, at least some of, them. We come to recognize that they, their point of view, and their cause deserve more consideration than we have previously been willing to give.

When we begin, then, to recognize glimpses of the full God-imaged createdness and humanity of every person regardless of race, ethnicity, gender, sexual identity, age, ableness or economic status, we can accord them the dignity and respect such recognition demands. Whether they are perceived as standing above or below us, in any measure, they can never be accorded the equality that authentic reconciliation demands if we envision them as anything less.

Yet, we must also develop the humility that allows us to begin to see every positive attribute we possess, either as individuals or as members of a social or cultural group, as a gift from God. These are never something for which we can legitimately claim special privilege.

Our cultural identity, race, gender, intellectual capacity, and "Every good thing given and every perfect gift [that is in us] is from above and comes down from the Father... "[89] We, therefore, have no bragging rights. We own nothing that has not been given to us, and all that has been invested in us is for service on behalf of the world that "God so loves."

This realization constrains us to, diligently and soberly, consider and obey the biblical admonition to,

> *Have this attitude in yourselves which was also in Christ Jesus, who… emptied Himself, taking the form of a bond-servant, and… humbled Himself by becoming obedient to the point of death*[90]

It is easy to convince ourselves that we are okay. It is easy to pride ourselves in our liberality in allowing each person their own space, in not bothering them—or allowing ourselves to be bothered by them. Our call to obedience, however, may lead us to actively work for the liberation of those in whom we hold no personal stake while recognizing that each of us, in some way, is a stakeholder in the other. For as poet John Donne so aptly pointed out, what diminishes any other member of the human family diminishes us.[91]

Acknowledgment

Coming to terms with the reality that the innate Will to Power can never be cured is sobering. Though its most debilitating symptoms can be restrained so that we are spared—and can spare others of the ugliness than is regularly unleashed. Such an urgent endeavor is a never-ending project, requiring diligence and willingness to confess

---

[89]Jas 1:17

[90]Phil 2:5-8a

[91]John Donne, "Meditation 17" in *The Works of John Donne. Vol III.,* Henry Alford, ed. London: John W. Parker, 1839. 574-5, 1624.

that we, too, have been culprits. For we are never far away from an irritating outbreak of the syndrome.

Acknowledging our complicity puts us on equal footing with the rest of God-created, yet fallen, humanity. As we honestly concede that it is not just "them" who have the problem, we are moved closer to God's intended intimate relationality. As we confess that it is not merely their negative attributes, way of life, or lack of Christian faith that deters intimate human relationship or extension of even a modicum of genuine respect, we can become serious about the prospect of weakening the Will to Power. And, in the end, if we are serious, we must concede that we have found the enemy and, at least in part, "it is us."

For despite protestations to the contrary, the deep-seated reach of the Will to Power will not allow us to neatly divide the world into camps of good and bad guys. Some may be more blatantly or explicitly guilty, yet we must confess that no one can completely resist the innate urge to perceive oneself as better—and more representative of the image of God—than, at least, one other person. No one has been fully able to, completely, avoid this common frailty. For, in its essence, it is inescapable.

All of us are, in some way, bad guys. We each, uniquely, and according to individual circumstances and proclivities, partake in the fallen nature that drives the exhibition of the Will to Power. This failing, along with our God-imaged createdness, makes us full participants in the human family, along with all others who desperately need to control someone.

From that simple acknowledgment, the possibility of genuine reconciliation, though tentative at best, comes into view. Still, we must also concede that the road to our goal is continually fraught with opportunities for missteps and faux pas that endanger the project. We are bound to misunderstand each other is some instances. We are bound to misspeak or be misheard. And, here, humility becomes enormously important. For we must always be ready to ask forgiveness rather than assert or pretend that the misstep is the other's fault. Only then, can we make progress and fend off the painful game of face off we play with each other.

Admitting that this is the best that we can do allows us to grant others grace when they fall short. It helps us understand that their powering – like ours – is not always deliberate or malicious but comes about because it is our shared disposition. Yet, none of us can, too easily, excuse ourselves for attitudes and actions that come about as the consequence of our Will to Power. None of us can escape. As brothers and sisters, we struggle together daily—moment by moment—to overcome an invincible disposition that can only be humbly acknowledged, recognized for what it is and repented of.

Repentance

The ultimate antidote, then, is living in a perpetual posture of repentance as the only viable way of restraining the Will to Power. We can never hold the other completely guilty while holding ourselves totally innocent. For a penitent posture requires conceding that nothing that the other has done to us is, individually or collectively, greater than what we have done to God.

The imperative of repentance of our lack of love for the other may not immediately be evident for we do not hate anyone. Still, our inclination to disregard them and deny their full humanity has caused them harm. Genuine repentance is most visibly represented in mature, agape love. The Apostle Paul inserts a seeming incongruous intrusion into one of his most often quoted passage when he inserts,

> *[w]hen I was a child, I used to speak like a child, think like a child, reason like a child; when I became a man, I did away with childish things.*[92]

---

[92]I Corinthians 13:11

Walking in an attitude of uninterrupted penitence requires growing up spiritually through a continual renewing of our mind that reflects on the other's lived reality until a change of attitude wards off the sin that "so easily besets" each of us. For the temptation to boast of our own innocence always lodges within us, ready to overtake us and to cause us to, again, give in to the Will to Power.

Paul's words, however, highlight the difference between immature and mature love, ingenuine and genuine charity. Immature, childish love seeks a return benefit for the one extending it. We love them for who they are—and what they provide—to us, whether it be the support and sustenance provided by a parent, the benefit of friendship offered by a playmate, the assistance given by a work colleague, or the emotional support and sexual gratification of a lover. They are there to aid, affirm, and comfort us and we love them for doing just that. When they no longer deliver these things, our love for them wanes.

Mature love is extended for the benefit of the other, and esteems him or her as a worthy recipient, regardless! As the Apostle insists, real love does not seek benefit for itself[93] and, as Jesus contends, is extended even to our enemy. For such mature love "does not take into account a wrong [that has been] suffered."[94] Mature love is deliberate and relentlessly vigilant about confronting the isms that creep into our minds and spirits. It determinately resists the temptation to base interactions on childish notions of what love is.

The Christian mandate for mutual servanthood and "submitting [our]selves one to another is a serious obligation.[95] Only mutual submission within the bounds of this mature love allows us to move the conversation from one of counter demands to one that hears what the other is authentically saying. and discerning their legitimate claims and grievances.

---

[93]I Corinthians 13:5

[94]Ibid.

[95]Eph 5:21

Repentance, however, is more than a confession of guilt, after being caught in the act or a fleeting sense of general remorse for the situation in which we find ourselves. Genuine repentance concedes that our attitudes and actions toward the other have been and continue to be, implicated in working out the Will to Power. It agrees with the other that we partake in systems that have caused their injury and leads us to intentionally find ways to assist in the remedy. Only such a posture represents true repentance for the damage that has been caused to the other.

Living intentionally, as if every person and every injustice mattered, is imperative. The task is to be deliberate about what we do and say. It involves us in conversation with those who are unlike us in some important, and potentially disarming, way. To hear—and not offhandedly dismiss—their humanity, their journey, or their pain. To purposely reach across barriers to establish, formerly untenable, relationships. To abstain from using privilege at the expense of others and initiate processes that accrue privilege to them. When we deliberately exchange our tendency toward Will to Power for these, seemingly unnatural, attitudes and actions, we move toward conquering our tendency just to be who we are and to allow others to go on as they are, to the detriment of both.

For this project to be successful, repentance and forgiveness must go hand in hand. While we repent of what we have done to them, we must forgive them for what they have done to us. The latter is no good without the former. The willingness to pardon is one of the surest signs of involvement in the Kingdom of God. For Jesus challenged us that unless we can forgive we have no claim as part of that Kingdom.[96]

The ability to forgive and still hold accountable is possibly one of the most difficult tasks we can be asked to take on. Forgiving does not mean holding the offender harmless or pretending no harm has been done. That is foolish naiveite. Neither is it dismissing or downplaying

---

[96]Mk 11:26

the extent of the real damage that has been caused. That would be self-delusion.

Forgiveness is not a free pass to intimate relationality. It does not require us to irresponsibly trust the offender to never again act in an unjust manner. Nor does it relieve the other's responsibility for owning and attempting to redress the harm they have caused. Though biblical forgiveness does not stop short when this acknowledgment is not forthcoming, the most authentic mode of forgiveness is reciprocal. We can only have genuine reconciliation and cease to be convinced that their overtures are ingenuine, after mutually embracing forgiveness. The imperative remains acknowledgment of deep-seated wounds their bigotry has caused and not dismissing claims of injury, while at the same time, accepting their overtures of genuine repentance.

It begins with intentionally entering into dialogue with others. Not just casual discussion, but quality conversation that allows us to comprehend their viewpoint and concedes their right to hold completely opposing convictions. They, in turn, have a responsibility to speak those convictions with passion—to speak their truth in love. We must speak with them—not at them about what we perceive as their problem, but about our common human experience. As we let down our guard about who we are, we allow them to do the same. Hopefully, this, in turn, allows both to approach the point where we share hopes, aspirations, struggles, and victories. As we, repeatedly, do this, we gradually become comfortable with each other and come to see each other as equal participants in our God-imaged createdness. Only after that can the conversation move to the issues that continue to separate us.

Within the Christian context, this process of deepening conversation calls for a democratization of the community of faith that creates a safe, affirming place where each person is equally valued for their gift. In such places, power, authority, and responsibility for cultivating a Kingdom paradigm can be shared. Each person—male and female, regardless of racial or ethnic identity, gender, age, degree of ableness, or socio-economic class can be accorded equal worth. Each can be invited fully into the Kingdom building project.

Repentance is more than empty words of quickly passing remorse. Rather, it involves a deep-seated conversion that urges us to actively seek to redress the brokenness of our communities that the Will to Power has engendered. Such repentance is not a magic elixir for all that ails us. And, certainly, it must be proceeded by recognition and acknowledgment, but it is the only viable way to begin to extricate ourselves from the desperate, devastating grip of the Will to Power.

CONCLUSION: JUSTICE AND RIGHTEOUSNESS

The conclusion, when all has been heard, is: fear God and keep His commandments, because this applies to every person Eccl 12:13

... let justice roll down like waters
And righteousness like an ever-flowing stream Amos 5:24

Shortly after the 9-1-1 terror incident of 2001, I was flying home from an engagement. In the airport waiting area, I encountered a group of seven or eight men who appeared to be Middle Eastern, dressed similarly in tan clothing, boarding my flight. They stood close enough to me that I could hear them speaking a language I did not understand. With the terror incident fresh in my mind, I began praying for God to protect the flight from any inclination these men might have to do something to endanger us. In the middle of my prayer, however, I was arrested by the sobering realization that I, who prided myself on being open to racial inclusion and equity, was a racist! Based solely on imbedded cultural cues of ethnicity, dress, and language, I had assumed that these men I did not know anything about might be up to some dangerous scheme. While the tension of the time, may have made my apprehension understandable to some, it does not erase the truth that we often are uneasy about those unlike ourselves based on far less explicit stimuli.

During that same period, while preparing for an assignment to assist with vacation Bible school, I listened to a cassette tape of children's Bible songs. I paid little attention, as I mindlessly sang along with the first stanza of the familiar song:

Jesus Loves the little children, all the children of the world,
Black and yellow, red and white, all are precious in his sight;
Jesus loves the little children of the world.

As the second stanza played, however, I was surprised by words which I had never heard, or paid attention to, before:

Jesus died for all the children, all the children of the world,
Black and yellow, red and white, all are precious in his sight;
Jesus died the little children of the world.

In the middle of that verse, the Holy Spirit seized my attention with the admonition, "that also means the Iraqi children"—the children of your enemies! At that time, many American citizens, including Christians, desired God's revenge on those who dared to, brazenly and viciously, attack our country. Like the Psalmist, they were praying that "their memory be cut off from the earth."[97] Yet, the message of that simple song reminded me that the Iraqi children were among all those children whom God so loves. They are as important to God—as precious in God's sight, as my own children, grandchildren, and all American or Christian children. Indeed, I had to acknowledge that Iraqi people and the nation of Iraq were part of the world that God so loved and for whom God sent his son. Taking such acknowledgment to its spiritual end, removes the felt right to power over them as if they were less reflective of God's image.

---

[97]Ps 109:15

Returning to Rodney King's original question, "Can we all get along," insistence on the need for social justice to prevail as the price for getting along is a scary, offensive proposition to many who live a comfortable life. Yet that question haunts those who crave a more just world for themselves as well as others.

The unfortunate politicizing of the term, justice, often leads to a Christian church divided between two poles. On the one hand, some have the irrational fear that anyone who passionately crusades for justice is radically subversive. Justice advocates are seen as not only undermining narrow national interests, but also thwarting the evangelistic project of the church as God's ultimate cause. On the other hand, those who are convinced that any Christian who does not actively advocate for justice at every turn is hypocritical, see those Christians as not only undermining the faith, but, ultimately, undermining God's entire prophetic project.

Unfortunately, these attitudes result in a false dichotomy between justice and righteousness in which either one is for a rigid standard of personal piety or an unyielding standard of social justice. We, mistakenly, see these commitments as a bifurcated, either/or proposition. Yet, the biblical witness indicates that it has never been so and promotes a both/and understanding of the Gospel.

Scripture's repeated use of the term, justice, indicates its import within the heart and mind of God. God not only expects God's people to be just, but God also sets standards for that justice, and reproves and judges those who do not live it out. Those who call themselves by God's name are expected to exhibit just attitudes and actions toward those whom they employ, those who are indebted to them, and with whom they transact commerce, as well as to the stranger. All these people are, in some way, the other, and yet God intended that the same justice—the same regard—that is shown to the neighbor be shown to them.

At the same time, God's requirement for personal righteousness is never to be neglected. For God also sets standards for living out a life that abstains from personal attitudes and actions, that, in any way, debase the clarity of the reflection of God's image within us or the other. Further, it is often the lack of our perceived personal holiness or what we perceive as that lack in the other that drives the Will to Power.

Still, King's primitively phrased, seemingly naïve, query speaks volumes about the complexity of relationships between people of differing races, cultures, classes, ages, and abilities, as well as among men and women. It focuses us on the reality that the plethora of our isms make it all but impossible for us to do what should be an easy task—to simply get along.

Our complex world regularly reminds us of how hard it is to peacefully co-exist without wishing or perpetrating ill will toward the other and leaves us with our queries: What makes it so hard to consider those of different races, cultures or genders truly our equals in every vital way? Why are the motivations and impulses of those of a different class, age group, economic status or gender identity viewed as suspect or considered inferior, when they have done nothing to warrant such attribution? And finally, what makes the task of social justice so complicated within the context of Christian society that gives, at least lip service, to the ideology of charity and fairness?

Again, neither victims nor perpetrators are entirely innocent. The victim does not merely want to cast off injustice, ameliorate the pain and live free. Rather, often they desire to trade places with the perpetrator and exact a penalty for that pain. Though we tell ourselves that we are more compassionate, loving, and God-like, if we could trade places with our oppressors, given the same options and opportunities, born into the same situation of privilege in one area or another, we would become them. We would exchange places to show them how it feels, at least for once, to be oppressed. We would inflict on them what they have inflicted on us. We want to teach them a lesson they will never forget. We want to extract retribution.

What we want is complete freedom from contact with the other. For fear of the other is the driving force behind the Will to Power. We are apprehensive that the other is both superior and inferior to us. This fear hinders us from ever encountering the other as created in the same image of God as we are. It keeps us from seeing those who are not physically, spiritually, or culturally identical to us—as equally part of that image. For doing that, we sense, requires negating ourselves and relinquishing, undeserved power to the other.

Finally, again, our failure to comprehend the depth of our fallenness blinds us to our situation. We cannot discern our deficiency in comprehending the other or Ultimate Reality. We are sure that they have a problem, for we easily see the most minute speck of imperfection in them from a far distance. Yet, we don't recognize that we also are imperfect. We are convinced that, somehow, we are more like God. For we continually fail to understand that the only perfect One *is* God. We fail to understand that to be human, by definition, is to be finite in every aspect, including our capacity to embrace the other.

If we recognized and acknowledged our common failing as participants in the human family, we are never surprised when earnest attempts at reconciliation fall short. Further, if we recognized and acknowledged its persistence—that from the beginning, this attitude has plagued humanity, stifling every attempt to create intimate community, we would be more realistic about what we could accomplish. We could be free to confront vestiges of the Will to Power when we discover them in ourselves, even knowing it can never be, thoroughly, dislodged.

The King incident reminds us of the many injustices: racism, sexism, classism, homo—and heterophobia, generationalism, ableism, nationalism, and economic oppression that saturate the socio-ethical fabric of our society. Whether they are played out as subtle undercurrents of discontent, in not so subtle, nuanced episodes of intolerance, or in the most radical and blatantly explosive episodes of rigid fanaticism, they rob us of the opportunity for the level of intimate relationality for which we were created.

On their face, these prejudices seem to have little in common, except that they dehumanize those subjected to them. Indeed, these biases, seemingly, are supported by vastly different presuppositions that, on their surface, have varying warrant. Injustice itself, in all its iterations, however, is the natural outworking of human fallenness. None of us completely separates ourselves from the tentacles of this insidious weed. For we have seen that, at its root, it stems from a singular, innate, sinful desire lodged in each of us as flawed, fallen humans to be better than at least one other person, group, or community.

Finally, then, the concept of Will to Power appropriately applies to every ism that exists. This conception sees all injustices as intertwined and, at their core, stemming from a single desire, innate in all human beings to be dominant over or better than someone else—anyone else. It exhibits itself in a variety of ways—not just economic or physical. It can also be social, emotional, mental, or spiritual. It can be personal, social, institutional, or systemic.

As we peel the layers of difference away to create, supposedly, authentic relations with those who entirely resemble us, we are left with an extremely limited circle. I am not white, so I cannot have intimate relationship with white people. I am not male, so I cannot fully entrust myself to a relationship with any male. I am not rich, so I have no dealings with those who have wealth. I am not poor; therefore, I stay away from those in want. I am not theologically liberal or politically conservative, so I distance myself from those who do not hold my unique position. I am not young, so I must stay away from younger generations. I am not gay or lesbian and so I must always be suspicious of their agenda.

When we finish separating ourselves from all those others who are psychically, socially, and spiritually different from us, however, we are left with a very tiny community of one. In that lonely and frightening place, we are always at odds with some segment of the human community and never entirely at peace with the rest of it. Indeed, this feeling of isolation is a potent weapon for creating a sense of despondency and depression that has fueled a pandemic rise in rates of mental illness, substance abuse, and suicide within contemporary society.

Intentional, as well as unintentional, discourses carry under and overtones of Will to Power. These unfortunate discourses are heard as much in public pronouncements as in intimate conversations. They are intoned in sermons, classroom lectures, political speeches, and media advertisements. Blatant as well as subliminal messages bombard us with the enticement to give into Will to Power at every turn. Such unfortunate rhetoric from both sides creates a stalemate that does nothing to settle our differences or move us closer to intended intimate relationality. "The enemy is them," these messages tell us. Their culture, values, attitudes, and actions stand against everything we are or hold to be decent and deserving of respect. So, we not only reject their request to simply co-exist in spaces that we have claimed as our own, we must prevent them from getting near us lest they overtake us.

As the opposite of love is not hate, the reverse of othering is not "saming" that denies or ignores the obvious differences that exist. Rather, to counter the rampant othering that destroys human community requires that we create climates of belonging that draw the other into the circle of human inclusiveness and celebrate the unique contributions of each person, group, culture, and society, while causing us to reexamine our isms.[98]

Opportunities are always present to privately, or openly, denounced vestiges of bigotry as they appear before us. And it is imperative to take every conceivable opportunity to actively work

---

[98]For an excellent exposition of this concept, see John A Powell, "Us vs Them: The Sinister Techniques of 'Othering' – And How to Avoid Them" *The Guardian* November 8. 2017.

toward restructuring institutions that promote or support bigotry in any form and to deconstruct institutions that cannot be reformed. For, in the end, the ultimate goal of reconciliation is not to return us to a pristine state that existed before the injustice. Neither is it to force the other into a binding agreement about our worldview or our assessment of them and their worldview. It is not even to assure some form of artificial equality. Rather, its ultimate goal is to return humanity to the intimate relationality God intended in Creation. Its project is opening the opportunity for every person to participate in reflecting the full image of God to each other member of the human community. To stop sort of this goal is to settle for less than God intended.

ABOUT THE AUTHOR

Estrelda Y. Alexander, a sociologist, political theologian, and minister is president of William Seymour College which she founded in 2010 and Executive Editor of Seymour Press, both in Lanham, Maryland. She is also an adjunct professor of theology at Seattle Pacific University and Virginia Union University. From 1998 until 2002, she served as Associate Dean of Community Life at Wesley Theological Seminary, leaving there to serve on the theology faculty at Regent University School of Divinity until 2013, rising to the rank of full professor.

Her published works include Black Fire: One Hundred Years of African American Pentecostalism; Black Fire Reader: A Documentary Resource on African American Pentecostalism; Limited Liberty: The Ministry and Legacy of Four Pentecostal Women Pioneers; and The Women of Azusa Street. She also co-edited two works (with Amos Yong) Phillip's Daughters: Women in the Pentecostal Movement and Afro-Pentecostalism: Black Pentecostal and Charismatic Christianity in History and Culture. Volume one of her three volume Dictionary of Pan African Pentecostalism was released this year. Additionally, she has authored more than thirty essays and journal articles.

Dr. Alexander has spoken in pulpits and college campuses across the United States. She received her B.A. in Sociology from Howard University, her M.A. in Sociology from Columbia University, her M.Div. from Wesley Theological Seminary, and her Ph.D. in Political Theology from The Catholic University of America.

Dr. Alexander is ordained in the Church of God (Cleveland, Tennessee), where she has served as a pastor and church planter as well as in various pastoral staff positions.

Bibliography

Butler, Robert Neil. Butler, "Age-ism: Another Form of Bigotry." *The Gerontologist* 9:4 (1969)., 243–246.

Busey, Christopher L. "Examining Race from Within: Black Intraracial Discrimination in Social Studies Curriculum" *Social Studies Research and Practice*. 9:2 (Summer 2014), 120-131.

Cone, James. *God of the Oppressed*. Maryknoll, NY: Orbis, 1977.

DeGruy, Joy. *Post Traumatic Slave Syndrome: America's Legacy of Enduring Injury and Healing*. s.l., DeGruy Publications, 2017.

Ellis, David. "LA Lawless" *Time Magazine,* May. 11, 1992.

Girard, Rene. *Violence and the Sacred*. Baltimore: Johns Hopkins University Press, 1977.

Gustavo Gutierrez, *A Theology of Liberation: History, Politics, and Salvation*. Maryknoll, NY: Orbis Books, 1988.

Hunter, Margaret. "The Persistent Problem of Colorism: Skin Tone, Status, and Inequality" *Sociology Compass*, (July 2007), 237–254.

King, Martin Luther. *Strength to Love*. New York: Pocket Books, 1964

Kristof, Nicholas D. and Sheryl WuDunn. *Half the Sky: Turning Oppression into Opportunity for Women Worldwide*. New York: Alfred A. Knopf, 2009.

Nelson, Todd D., ed. *Ageism: Stereotyping and Prejudice Against Older Persons.* MIT Press, 2004.

Nietzsche, Friedrich. *Beyond Good and Evil: Prelude to a Philosophy of the Future*. New York: The MacMillan Company, 1907.

__________________. *The Will to Power.* R. Kevin Hill and Michael A. Scarpitti. Trans, New York: Penguin Books, 2017.

Salter McNeil, Brenda. *Roadmap To Reconciliation: Moving Communities into Unity, Wholeness and Justice*. Downers Grove, IL: InterVarsity Press, 2015.

Sanders, Cheryl. *Empowerment Ethics For a Liberated People: A Path to African American Social Transformation.* Minneapolis, MN: Fortress Press, 1995

Schelling, Thomas. *Micromotives and Macrobehavior*, Revised Edition. New York: W. W. Norton & Company, 2006.

Volf, Miraslov. *Exclusion and Embrace: A Theological Exploration of Identity, Togetherness, and Reconciliation.* Nashville, TN: Abingdon Press, 1996.

Index

CPSIA information can be obtained
at www.ICGtesting.com
Printed in the USA
LVHW030912180820
663383LV00003B/213

9 781938 373398